· *BUILDING* ·
· *DOMESTIC* ·
· *LIBERTY* ·

· BUILDING ·
· DOMESTIC ·
· LIBERTY ·

Charlotte Perkins Gilman's
Architectural
Feminism

POLLY WYNN ALLEN

The University of Massachusetts Press

Amherst

1988

Library of Congress Cataloging-in-Publication Data

Allen, Polly Wynn, 1936–
Building domestic liberty : Charlotte Perkins Gilman's
architectural feminism / Polly Wynn Allen.

p.   cm.

Bibliography: p.

Includes index.

ISBN 0–87023–627–X (alk. paper). ISBN 0–87023–628–8
(pbk. : alk. paper)

1. Gilman, Charlotte Perkins, 1860–1935—Political and social
views. 2. Feminism and literature–United States. 3. Women in
literature. 4. Architecture, Domestic, in literature. 5. Space
(Architecture) in literature. 6. Home in literature. 7. Sex role
in literature. 8. Domestic fiction, American—History and
criticism. I. Title.

PS1744.G57Z54 1988   87–35311
818'.409—dc19   CIP

British Library Cataloguing in Publication data are available

Frontispiece. Unsigned photograph of Charlotte Perkins Gilman, from
about 1905.

Unless otherwise noted, all pictorial material is from the Schlesinger
Library, Radcliffe College, Cambridge, Massachusetts. Grateful
acknowledgment is made for permission to use it here.

Contents

Preface   vii

Introduction   3

One · The Social Landscape in Gilman's Day   9

The Industrial Transformation of Production   11
Technology and the Home   13
Ideology Prescribes Domestic Womanhood   15
Breaking Out of Compulsory Domesticity   16
The Material Feminist Tradition   20
Revisiting the Optimism of the Progressive Era   25

Two · Who Was Charlotte Perkins Gilman?   27

A Feminist/Socialist with a Mission   29
An Unconventional Youth   31
Marriage, Motherhood, and Melancholia: Walter, Katharine, and
Divorce   37
Writer and Public Speaker: Launching a Career in California   39
Wife Again: Houghton, Career, Fulfillment, and Disillusionment   45
Cancer Victim: Impending Death and Premeditated Suicide   54

*Three · Gilman's Attention to Domestic Architecture: Her Fourfold Case
against Prevailing Household Design*   55

The Fruit of Gilman's Experience of "Home"   57
The Scope of Gilman's Case against Conventional Housing Design   60
Gilman's Four-Count Indictment against the Organization of the Home   62
Evaluating the Power of Gilman's Indictment   77

Contents

Four · Gilman's Utopian Portrait of Nonsexist Landscapes   81

Gilman's Introduction to the Architectural Imagination   83
Utopia in Four Stories: Futuristic New York City, California, and
Herland   88
Gilman's Composite Utopia   99

Five · Gilman's Pragmatic Approach to Neighborhood Design   103

New Media for a Feminist/Socialist Message   105
Discussing Design Specifications in Popular Magazines and
Newspapers   105
What Diantha Did   114
Gilman's Strategy for Changing the Built Environment   115

Six · Gilman's Philosophy of World Improvement Led by Women   119

Social Unity as the Foundation for Social Ethics   121
Glory to Growth in the Highest   126
Women as Agents of Social Salvation   130
Theoretical Gridlock   140

Seven · The Power of Gilman's Storytelling Voice   143

Models of Feminist Architecture in Gilman's Tales   146
The Importance of Stories to Gilman's Vision   162

Eight · Conclusion   165

Gilman's Influence in a Changing World   167
Beyond Gilman's Intellectual and Political Gridlock   171
Building Women-Supporting Neighborhoods   175

Notes   179

Index   191

Preface

Fifty-three years after Charlotte Gilman's death, too many people still face mind-boggling difficulties in balancing their daily lives between work and family obligations. In almost every case, they do so without benefit of residences or neighborhoods built to Gilman's feminist/socialist design specifications. Her turn-of-the-century architectural analysis of work-place/home-place antagonisms, although seriously flawed, contains much insight that is enduringly shrewd and suggestive. Her vision of an alternative, woman-supporting landscape remains powerful enough to arrest the attention of would-be planners, developers, and community activists as the end of another century approaches.

I wrote this book primarily for two overlapping groups. One is made up of people who think it is important, as part of the process of achieving personal integrity, to understand the stories of people like themselves in ages past, including their warts and their triumphs. The other consists of those who believe both that every person has a right to decent housing and that neighborhood residents have a right to help determine the design of their natural and built environments. Because I belong to both groups, it is true to say that I wrote the book for myself.

Hungry to know the long-neglected history of women and other subordinate groups, I have been personally rewarded by becoming well acquainted with Charlotte Gilman. She died just fourteen months before I was born, and I have had a strong sense of being able almost to touch her historically. Because I am committed to joining forces with others, women and men, who advocate, agitate, and organize to build affordable, appropriate housing, the project of setting forth Gilman's architectural legacy has been both delightful and frustrating.

While I have enjoyed the vitality of Gilman's architectural imagination, I have never stopped bemoaning the present lack of women-supporting built environments. Like Gilman, I have spent long years at my typewriter (in my case mostly a word processor) which has required me to slight related political matters that are very important to me. Although communication with people who are actually building alternative neighborhoods has been and remains gratifying, I expect that getting my own hands dirtier in the days ahead will be even more satisfying.

I want to thank five groups of people for their role in the creation of this book. In the first instance, professional historians, sociologists, academics from several other fields, and librarians have assisted me over the years by sharing their work, their encouragement, and their criticisms. Professor Carl Degler started the modern revival of interest in Charlotte Gilman with his essay "Charlotte Perkins Gilman on the Theory and Practice of Feminism" (*American Quarterly,* Spring 1956, pp. 21–39) and his subsequent agency in republishing Gilman's *Women and Economics.* Jill Conway, Ann Swidler, Theda Skocpol, Arthur Dyck, and Preston Williams advised me during my work's initial appearance as a Ph.D. dissertation ("The Social Ethics of Charlotte Perkins Gilman." Harvard University, 1978). Mary Hill and Ann Lane, fellow Gilman scholars, conferred with me generously at an early stage. Diana Royce of the Nook Farm Research Library in Hartford, Connecticut, and Barbara Haber, Eva Moseley, Marie-Hélène Gold, Susan von Salis, and Cynthia Law of the Schlesinger Library in Cambridge, Massachusetts, assisted my research efforts with grace and skill; Moseley's pithy summary of the Gilman Papers, the entirety of which she cataloged in the early 1970s, remains remarkably rich and succinct. My associates in the Mellon project on Women and Social Change at Smith College in the early 1980s were supportively attentive at an important moment in my life; Sharon Pollack, Ruth Banta, and Suzanne Marilley, in particular, contributed important insight and research cooperation. Recently Joyce Berkman and Myrna Breitbart, by their careful reading of the entire manuscript, have helped me very substantially to improve it. Through her scholarship, her engagement in hands-on building, and her hope for my project, Dolores Hayden has been a special inspiration to me throughout.

In the second instance, two relatives and a one-time neighbor of Charlotte Gilman have added a dimension of historical immediacy to my studies, which I have very much appreciated. Dorothy Stetson Chamberlin, Gilman's granddaughter, welcomed me to Pasadena in December 1979, chauffering me through a labyrinth of highways in her colorful (ancient) Jeep and letting me wander respectfully through the small frame house where Gilman spent her last days. On the same trip, Thomas

Gardiner Perkins, Gilman's nephew, received me warmly at his Pasadena home. He described his Aunt Charlotte's style of telling Bible stories, which included common-sense "annotations" to demonstrate their de-mythologized meanings. In the summer of 1983, Eleanor Barrie, who lives on Washington Street in Norwich Town, Connecticut, kindly shared girlhood memories of playing croquet in the summertime with her jolly next-door neighbor, Charlotte Gilman.

Undoubtedly I could not have finished this project without the Office of Information Technology at Harvard University and its very capable, hard-working staff. I thank all the gentle people who persuaded me I could learn word processing: Zack Deal, who taught me and solved many nettlesome problems for me; everyone who answered my questions and carefully maintained the facility day after day; Rita Mahoney and Eda Stockson, who manage the office's financial infrastructures; all the "user assistants" who cheerfully helped me when I became stuck; Bob Ross, Bob Weber, Pauline Dunson, and Tony Vagnucci, who became my comrades in a common adventure; and finally, a rousing cheer for the friendly main-frame computer, for remembering and forgetting at my command. What a comfort!

In the fourth instance, I want to thank the staff of the University of Massachusetts Press for their competent shepherding of my manuscript. Dick Martin liked it and shared his enthusiasm effectively. Barbara Palmer and Pam Wilkinson copy edited it creatively and meticulously. Catlin Murphy took a special, informed interest in promoting it. Barbara Werden skillfully designed it. For these and the management of a myriad other production details, I am grateful.

Finally, members of my family and close friends have cared for me and this project in touching, tangible ways. At an early stage, Karen Smyers collaborated with me both in Gilman research and in my own child-care responsibilites. Ann Henaff, Anne Ryle, Neal Blanton, Dorothy Green, Mary McFeeley, Ann Bookman, and Liv Pertzoff took the time to read either selected chapters or the whole manuscript carefully and to give me their critical response. Other friends have talked with me about the project in supportive, constructive ways through the years, most notably Judy Misterka, Cheryl Clark, Jan Peterson, Judy Hikes, Tina Bowman, Chris Weller, Bill Cavellini, Mary Shepherd, Susan Bizzell, Cathy Topal, Susan Tobias, Carolyn Arnold, Brett Averit, Susan Stuebing, Julia Wallace, Jim Wallace, Betty Sawyer, Art Kimber, Joan Kimber, Suzanne Weber,

Ruth Hawkins, Bruce Hawkins, Patrick Henaff, Joan Mark, and Alex Pertzoff. For almost a decade, my two sons have made room in our family for Charlotte Gilman with impressive patience, grace, and support. John Samuel Robinson, my elder son, conspired with me in naming the book; David Wynn Robinson, my younger son, took the author's photo on the cover and made the drawing found at page 95. I thank you all.

· *BUILDING* ·
· *DOMESTIC* ·
· *LIBERTY* ·

Introduction

We need a different environment, and we shall never come into
smooth, peaceful, richly productive life until we have it.

CHARLOTTE PERKINS GILMAN
1916

Charlotte Gilman believed that women would remain subservient to men as long as the architectural setting of family life required them to do large quantities of solitary domestic work. She advocated the rearrangement of the built environment as the most sensible way to resolve the agonizing conflicts adults face between the claims of family and those of paid work. By virtue of its practical integration of the realms of domesticity and employment, the feminist architecture she recommended would allow women at last to assume their rightful place as equal citizens and workers in society at large.

Gilman had a lively appreciation of the importance of spatial design to gender relationships. She analyzed the negative effects of prevailing domestic architecture, with its private systems of food preparation, laundering, child care, and cleaning, on men, women, and children. She characterized the middle-class housewife's familial responsibilites as "a quiet, unnoticed whirlpool that sucks down youth and beauty and enthusiasm."[1] She lamented the isolated alienation of many women's lives, depicting the endless cooking and cleaning of things as the highly stressed "systole and diastole of the domestic heart."[2] She wanted a greater variety of residential options, ones that would link built private spaces with shared facilities housing all the necessary domestic services. In a vivid way she recognized that the built environment could facilitate rather than thwart the convenient combination of outside work with family responsibilites. Throughout her life, she cherished a vision of domestic liberty for all people.

In 1975 Gilman's analysis of middle-class domestic life reached across the decades and laid a claim on me. Encountering her toward the end of a doctoral program in religious studies, my admiration was initially aroused by Gilman's bold critique of sexism in theological language. The strength of her commitment to economic independence for married women intensified the connection. Finally, her architectural approach, both to the status quo in gender relations and to the struggle for an alternative future, spoke to my own domestic circumstances in a deeply existential way. Over the ensuing years, my efforts to understand Gilman have required (and helped) me to pay attention to "unnoticed whirlpools" of distress in my own life, one result of which is a decidedly healthier heartbeat.

Partly learned from others and partly original, the three-dimensional perspective that Gilman developed can be seen as a precursor to an emerging field in contemporary urban and women's studies, variously known as the geography of gender, community architecture, or women and environments. She spoke and wrote extensively at the turn of the twentieth century about the injustice and waste of conventional housing arrangements. In addition to her several book-length studies, she published dozens of shorter articles in magazines such as *Cosmopolitan, McCall's,* and *Harpers' Bazaar* to persuade a mass audience to change the design of its neighborhoods. To further her goals, she created and sustained her own monthly magazine, *The Forerunner,* from 1909 until 1916. In short stories and novels she set forth an extensive fictional realm, the physical settings of which were designed to accommodate a dignified balance of paid work and rejuvenating leisure equally for women and for men.

In focusing on the built settings for daily life, Gilman called for a unified approach to housework struggles and workplace struggles. She recognized that the layout of physical spaces is both arbitrary and political, thus alerting people to the environmental dimension of their efforts to harmonize family and job. Her critical analysis of conventional housing design is probably the most extensive ever undertaken from a feminist perspective. Drawing on the ideas of a variety of nineteenth-century socialists and feminists, she put together an eclectic vision of alternative landscapes in which workplace and home were closely situated and mutually supportive. Along with her mentors and colleagues, she urged people to find architectural remedies for women's "double shift" of housekeeping and paid work.

In versatile ways, Gilman set forth the message that domestic circumstances are a serious moral/political concern, a social problem deserving a coordinated public solution. Her stories as well as her exhortations to builders have the power to penetrate contemporary circumstances with searching questions about more egalitarian, supportive environmental designs.

Despite the remarkable energy she devoted to her architectural vision, Gilman herself doubted its value. She did not adequately trust her own spatial insights. A subject as lowly as the conduct of housework, she reckoned, was not worthy to stand as her principal life work. She was driven to do something more intellectually grand. Although she returned again and again to the nettlesome conundrums of domestic life, she regarded her sociology of household organization as less serious, less momentous, less enduring than her theology of world improvement. To that idealistic project she devoted her most extensive, concentrated labors.

Although she had learned experientially the role of the built environment in determining mobility, community, and other measures of liberty, Gilman downplayed the importance of that discovery in her own self-evaluation. She judged that her efforts at comprehensive theory in the fields of economics and ethics were her crowning (if unfinished) achievement. "Social economics and social ethics," she wrote, "—on those two I would rest my claim to social service."[3] Approached as a whole, Gilman's scholarly, often verbose, style has had the effect of overshadowing the crisp clarity of her focus on domestic arrangements.

In addition to her vaunted theoretical ambitions, Gilman was afflicted as an adult by extreme fluctuations in self-confidence. After suffering a severe emotional collapse in her mid-twenties, she continued intermittently to experience acute episodes of depressive melancholia. She characterized her mind during these periods as effectively equivalent to "a piece of boiled spinach," claiming that her crippled condition had robbed her of "twenty-seven adult years" of productivity.[4] For complex psychological reasons, she tried, over and over again, to justify her existence by writing a philosophical system that would eliminate sexism and selfishness from the world by changing people's ethical ideas.

Gilman's case for socialized neighborhood architecture grounded her moral passion and rendered it intelligible. In straining to express her zeal in an abstract, universalistic idiom, she lost touch with the particular truths of her own life and thus her capacity for connecting with other people's truths. Laboring with an elitist sense of calling, she wrote her formal ethics in a highly solitary, pretentious manner. Although she was unusually articulate, bold, and well-read, her heavy sense of moral mission was directed, condescendingly, at helping other people. As a proponent of radical changes in the built environment, however, she was never an aloof, intellectual expert trying to lift society by means of clever conceptual manipulations. She was an unabashedly interested party, determined to join forces with others in banishing domestic evil and improving the world, starting with the home.

CHAPTER ONE

The Social Landscape in Gilman's Day

Fairer far the hills should stand
Crownèd with a city's halls,
With the glimmer of white walls,
With the climbing grace of towers;
Fair with great fronts tall and grand,
Stately streets that meet the sky,
Lovely roof-lines, low and high,—
Fairer for the days and hours.

Woman's beauty fades and flies,
In the passing of the years,
With the falling of the tears,
With the lines of toil and stress;
City's beauty never dies,—
Never while her people know
How to love and honor so
Her immortal loveliness.

"City's Beauty"
CHARLOTTE PERKINS STETSON

THE INDUSTRIAL TRANSFORMATION OF PRODUCTION

The landscape of family life changed dramatically in the nineteenth century. The transition from a predominantly agrarian culture to an increasingly industrial one posed a stunning variety of life-style challenges. According to E. P. Thompson, the Industrial Revolution permanently "destroyed the balance between rural and urban life" in Great Britain.[1] Similar forces were at work in the United States, although the immense size of the continent was a mitigating factor for many decades. In response to new economic and demographic realities, U.S. families improvised a variety of strategies. One result was a geometrical expansion in the middle-class segment of the population.

Charlotte Gilman's parents and grandparents witnessed firsthand the transformation of the productive landscape in New England. Most families living around 1800 still produced the lion's share of household necessities for their own use. Besides growing food and livestock, the family was typically engaged in the domestic manufacture of the staples of everyday life, items such as yard goods, clothing, shoes, candles, and brooms. What few things they did not make for themselves were bartered or bought in nearby villages with the surplus of their own agriculture or craft. At the turn of the nineteenth century, when Gilman's great-aunts, Catharine and Harriet Beecher, were little girls, family and economic life for most Americans was indivisible, both spatially and culturally.

Economists frequently speak of the preindustrial phase of economic life as mercantile (or commercial) capitalism, referring to the practice of family members producing extra goods in their homes to sell for cash. Starting in colonial times, certain families had expressed the entrepreneurial spirit by expanding the volume of their household production. While Gilman's parents were children, patterns of surplus manufacture at home for market exchange were still widely seen. As they had for several generations, male artisans were commonly making shoes, pewter, and iron products to sell while female artisans were weaving extra cloth and making hats, clothing, and food for the same purpose.[2] Increasingly, merchants from outside the family would "give out" quotas of agricultural and manufacturing work to family members, later exchanging their finished products commercially for a profit. Although family members under mercantile capitalism had widening relations with sometimes distant markets, their daily life was still spatially centered in a common household.

Factory production was the most novel organizational development of social and economic life in the nineteenth century. Begun with the manufacture of textiles in New England at the end of the eighteenth century, the industrial shop had seriously challenged the family system of production by the time Gilman was born in 1860. By 1885, a process that displaced all but the necessary domestic industries from the home to the factory was virtually complete.[3]

Encouraged by national leaders who advocated industrial growth to match that of western Europe, people with capital had been building factories and furnishing them with heavy machinery for mass production throughout the nineteenth century. Owners had then proceeded to hire every worker they could lure away from their household shops. Hiring women workers, whom Alice Kessler-Harris has called "the first industrial proletariat," had particular advantages to labor-hungry manufacturers because women were not as tied to cycles of plowing and harvest as were their fathers and brothers.[4]

Toward midcentury, as the factory system expanded, employers discovered that they could simultaneously increase production, lower prices, and reap larger profits. Especially in growing urban areas, commercial household production could no longer compete. As early as the 1830s there were not enough native-born workers willing to toil eleven and twelve hours a day (or longer) for meager wages. As a result, manufacturers turned for cheap labor to large incoming waves of immigrant workers, beginning around 1840.[5] By the middle of the nineteenth century, roughly one-third of American women entered the paid labor force on a temporary basis, usually until they married. Only the poorest women—immigrants, widows, and free blacks—engaged in a lifelong effort to make ends meet financially by working outside of their homes.

Because of industrializing, urbanizing pressures, the matrix of social relations had become much more complex by 1860. No longer represented in the dominant culture as a web of interlocking families, society was seen on the eve of the Civil War more as "a conglomeration of detached individuals." Instead of a microcosm of society at large, the American family had become "a launching pad into the world" of competitive individualism.[6]

All these changes in the organization of economic life had a profound impact on relations within families. Whereas husband and wife were obviously dependent upon one another economically in more agrarian times, and their children equally dependent upon both, industrial production drove a variety of wedges between family members.[7] For one thing, the factory system separated individuals' work locations and daily schedules from those of others in the family; men, women, and children of one household no longer had the traditional satisfactions of working side by side in an unarguably common venture. For another, the culture generated by a growing and prosperous urban middle class exaggerated gender differences in extreme ways, assigning altogether distinctive roles to men and women; no longer husband and wife as economic partners, popular wisdom began to insist that woman was the economic dependent of her husband, by divine decree, and that she should stay at home while he went out to work.

During Charlotte Gilman's youth, the pace of mechanization intensified, stimulated in the North by the mobilization for civil war. In their determination to streamline production, manufacturers were dividing labor processes into smaller and smaller units (and thus "deskilling" their employees) in order to enhance both worker efficiency and management control. To increase their profits by beating out both national and international competitors, employers tried to keep their labor costs to a minimum. Low wages, sex stereotyping, and union breaking were but three of the management techniques that accelerated the immiserization of the ethnically diverse, increasingly female work force.

The last three decades of the nineteenth century were marked by the centralization of major industries, the consolidation of large fortunes by a few families, and the frantic search by these combined corporations for secure, ever-enlarging consumer markets. An eclectic radical movement arose in the 1880s, composed of miners, trade unionists, farmers, writers, and activists with a variety of concerns, to protest child labor, gigantic accumulations of wealth, colonial wars, and the mistreatment of women and other workers. Despite their heroic efforts and even the occasional massacre of protesters, monopoly capitalism, with its imperialist trends and increasingly international systems of finance and control, was fast becoming the economic setting for American family life by the turn of the twentieth century.

TECHNOLOGY AND THE HOME

The late-nineteenth-century acceleration of mechanical innovation had many applications for the conduct of housework. Almost all the early inventions designed for modernizing domestic labor were first built for use on a scale much larger than that of the individual household. Washing machines, refrigerators, dishwashers, and new kinds of stoves, for example, were originally built for use in commercial laundries, hospitals, hotels, and apartment houses. After the most affluent urban families were able to have their homes connected to gas, electricity, and running water in the 1880s, the prospect of more and more homes with plentiful water and energy supplies inspired the invention of a small power motor in 1889. Soon thereafter well-to-do individual households could purchase motor-driven appliances scaled for the private kitchen or parlor.[8]

Despite these mechanical inventions, most American women continued to wrestle with a very strenuous daily schedule of domestic chores. Providing three meals a day, for example, especially outside cosmopolitan urban areas, involved staggering hours of effort 365 days a year. Besides killing and plucking chickens, curing meat, and scaling fish for the table, American women grappled with challenges in the preparation of every item on their menus. The following list of routine household operations suggests the hard labor involved in late-nineteenth-century food preparation. "Roasting and grinding green coffee, grinding and sifting whole spices, cutting and pounding lump or loaf sugar, sifting heavy flour that might be full of impurities, soaking oatmeal overnight, shelling nuts, grinding cocoa shells, seeding raisins, making and nurturing yeast, drying herbs."[9]

In addition, doing laundry required the repeated fetching, carrying, heating, and disposing of water, with much bending, rubbing, and wringing; consuming long days and the labors of several, it left arms and backs aching and fingers raw. Alice Kessler-Harris reports that urban middle-class households commonly sent out their laundry to commerical establishments between 1870 and 1910.[10]

One hundred years ago, most women conducted their nurturing operations of feeding and cleaning equipped only with pails, tubs, fireplaces, hand tools, and, toward the end of the century, iron stoves that burned coal and/or wood. Most got along without refrigeration except for improvised arrangements such as barrels in the basement or burial places in the snow. Having no refrigerator usually entailed a daily trip to the market.

As always, the rigors of family-life maintenance were compounded with particular hardships for working-class women during the period under discussion. Many a woman had to work ten to twelve hours a day, six days a week, to earn wages sufficient to purchase such ready-made items as bread, canned food, and men's clothing, which she could no longer afford to produce at home. She had to organize her second shift of mending, food preparation, and cleaning around the edges of her paid work. Poor immigrant families made up as much as one-half of the population in several major cities by 1900. It was common for such cities to provide working-class neighborhoods with far fewer and less dependable public services than those available in middle-class areas. Thus working-class homemakers struggled against far greater quantities of dirt, grime, and accumulated refuse in houses that were usually very crowded and lacking in even the most basic bourgeois amenities.[11]

The expanding capitalist economy needed the home as a market for industrially produced goods. No longer having its own obvious productive importance, the home had begun to function as a satellite to the money economy. In the public imagination, the economic significance of the home shrank to its capacity to consume, measured by the extent of its buying power. Instead of the primary setting for the manufacture of necessary goods, the home was seen increasingly as merely one critical segment of the purchasing public.

IDEOLOGY PRESCRIBES DOMESTIC WOMANHOOD

An elaborate ideology of the middle-class family was created in the first half of the nineteenth century to rationalize the socioeconomic shifts that were taking place. This domestic code maintained that it was appropriate for men but not for women to leave home in pursuit of wages. It was built on the conviction that "the home required women's moral and spiritual presence" on a full-time basis.[12] Articulated in sermons, religious tracts, women's magazines, housekeeping manuals, and novels, it addressed the anxiety and guilt aroused by the culture's increasing preoccupation with material gain. It soothed the collective conscience by designating woman as the homebound representative of such traditional values as spirituality, interpersonal warmth, and home-centeredness.[13] It explained the apparent uncoupling of economic significance from the home by sentimentalizing woman's place within it. It characterized the strenuous processes of feeding, cleaning, and nurturing people as something other than socially valuable labor, classifying them not as "work" but rather as the natural expression of woman's inherently giving, nurturant character.

Gilman's great-aunt, Catharine Beecher, played a major role in formulating this "pact" of separate spheres. In her biography of Beecher,

Kathryn Sklar describes the compensatory bargain represented by the cult of woman-and-home: "If women would agree to limit their participation in the society as a whole . . . then they could ascend to total hegemony over the domestic sphere."[14] Celebrating the benevolent influence of woman through her sovereignty in the home, Beecher's voluminous writings about women, education, and domesticity imbued the conception of two separate gender worlds with considerable moral authority.

This ideology, often designated "the cult of domesticity," decreed that women had no place in the industrial work force. It subtly camouflaged the exploitation of women's unpaid labor in the home. It spoke of society in terms of two separate spheres: man's dangerous, public realm outside, and woman's safe, private realm inside, the four walls of home. It ordained women to be purifying agents of family stability by carrying out their timeless roles as wives and mothers enclosed within the boundaries of domestic space. What it obscured about the economic value of women's family roles in the home it attempted to compensate rhetorically, paying tribute to the alleged selflessness, delicacy, and intrinsic domesticity of women. Inattentive to the connection between women's unpaid domestic labor and the increasing profit margins of factory owners, it euphemistically crowned Mother "queen of the household empire."[15]

Nineteenth-century domestic ideology widened the cultural gulf between women of differing economic means. In venerating the private residence where woman was ideologically enthroned, the middle-class family code cast aspersions on women whose circumstances required that they leave home to work for wages, depicting them as a veritable "outcast group."[16] Oblivious to the economic realities driving poorer women out of the home, "the cult of domesticity" generated a deep sense of guilt and inferiority in family women who required their meager outside wages in order to survive. Adding insult to injury, the middle-class ideology admonished families to keep themselves apart from heterogeneous society, safely ensconced at home against the inevitable contamination of contact with the lower classes.[17]

BREAKING OUT OF COMPULSORY DOMESTICITY

Throughout the major part of the nineteenth century, a substantial number of white middle-class American women were disinclined to swallow pious platitudes calling for their demure detention in radically transformed domestic spaces. For at least six decades, leaders of the "woman movement" insisted, in Mary P. Ryan's amusing paraphrase, that "a sphere is not a home."[18] First aroused by their political powerlessness when working for the abolition of slavery, Lucretia Mott and Elizabeth Cady Stanton convened the first major assembly devoted to women's rights at Seneca Falls, New York, in 1848. With her long-standing collaborator, Susan B. Anthony, Stanton went on to organize the first national association explicitly concerned with gaining women's political equality, the National Woman Suffrage Association. In the 1870s and 1880s, Frances Willard, described by Mari Jo Buhle as the nineteenth century's "most influential and revered American woman," transformed the National Woman's Christian Temperance Union into a comprehensive social movement concerned with the rights of labor and of women, as well as the evils of Old Man Rum.[19] Willard's close friend, Mary Rice Livermore, also a fighter for suffrage and temperance, devoted her remarkable skills as a lecturer and journalist to the related causes of Christian socialism and economic independence for women.

After the Civil War, hundreds of thousands of women throughout the United States organized themselves into independent women's clubs, an organizational form that Buhle notes was "radical for the time." The purpose of a typical white club was twofold: to help middle-class women stand on their own two feet financially, and to advance various social and political reforms. Buhle notes that giving assistance to lower-class women who were looking for work was a consistent priority in these clubs. She insists that the popular image of women's clubs as dilettantish is false. In the eyes of a nineteenth-century clubwoman, "Meaningful club activities . . . had definite practical applications." By the late 1880s, woman's right to labor had become a cardinal tenet of the club movement.[20]

In an impressive challenge to the "two sphere" ideology of American family life, white clubwomen in the nineteenth century insisted that their work was "municipal" and not merely "private" housekeeping. Club organizing efforts addressed a wide variety of concerns, including conservation issues such as land use and sewage, family problems such as child labor and juvenile courts, factory abuses such as poverty wages and dawn-to-dark workdays, and women's rights matters such as coeducation and suffrage.[21] Julia Ward Howe, Mary Livermore, and later Charlotte Perkins Gilman were frequent guest lecturers to women's clubs all over the United States. On such occasions Gilman was fond of asking rhetorically,

"Shall the home be our world? or the world our home?" Making the whole wide world more "homelike" was a characteristic way of viewing the central vocation of the women's club.

Not all of the ideas being expressed within white women's clubs were progressive ones. Reinforced by scholarly work in anthropology and psychology, racism and nativism acquired considerable respectability in the last decades of the nineteenth century. A pervasive ideology of Anglo-Saxon hegemony maintained that there were inferior and superior races, that superior races produced higher cultures, and that the "amalgamation" of superior and inferior races would bring about the deterioration of the superior race and its loftier culture. By their hospitality to eugenicist theories, confusing their own intention to "improve the world" with the eugenicist imperative to "improve the race," some clubwomen seriously compromised the values of pluralistic democracy. Troubled by the influx of aliens to their cities, clubwomen were unfortunately not the only Americans invoking such ideas in support of their claims to nativistic social control.

Ancient Society, the popular 1878 work by cultural anthropoligist Lewis Henry Morgan, was very widely appropriated at the turn of the century as a racist interpretive device. Based on his field contact with the Iroquois of New York State, Morgan created a scheme of the entire span of human history, an outline that exerted tremendous influence both in scholarly and in reform circles. His representation distinguished seven successive cultural stages in three broad epochs; according to his theory, these eras and periods marked the invariant route from ancient antiquity to the present. With great authority, Morgan portrayed three great chapters in the history of the world, Savagery, Barbarism, and Civilization. His book was avidly studied both in classrooms and in clubs. At the same time, it was used by a variety of racists, including intellectuals at prominent universities, to demonstrate the relative depravity of non-Anglo-Saxon peoples.

Many white middle-class women's clubs had strong links with the socialist as well as the women's movements. In the 1880s and 1890s, there was a growing consensus on the left that the increasingly monopolistic tendency of business was so evil that American society would have to be completely reorganized along cooperative lines. As an important segment of the middle-class reform community, clubwomen both applauded the increasing militancy of the trade union movement and initiated thousands of ameliorative projects of their own. As the Socialist Labor party (and, after 1901, the Socialist party) gained organizing momentum and electoral credibility, nonpartisan socialists throughout the country were feeling profoundly optimistic about the prospects for nonviolent, democratic revolution. In the euphoric atmosphere of progressive community life, women and men of good will set out to transform every imperfect aspect of their dynamic society.

Socialists who worked for the party and socialists who worked outside the party in strictly educational campaigns shared the goal of banishing scandalous extremes of wealth and poverty. Convinced that everyone could and should enjoy a fair share of national prosperity, they labored in their several ways to bring down the mighty and lift up the downtrodden. Utopian socialists removed from daily working-class concerns were the most likely of the anticapitalists to entertain the illusion that wealthy people could be persuaded voluntarily to relinquish their assets for distribution among the poor.

Nonpartisan socialists in particular liked to mute rather than foster class consciousness; they regarded Karl Marx as excessively negative about structural antagonisms between owners and workers. A typical women's club was concerned as much about capitalism's injury to the idle rich woman as it was about its exploitation of the worker. Whereas women on the left were united against the tangible suffering of the masses laboring in factories, they were similarly resolute against the spiritual poisoning of middle-class women banished from paid labor. In the ethos of the white women's club, the worker's right to a just wage and decent working conditions was matched in importance by the right of the middle-class woman to meaningful labor.

The early women's clubs were strongly committed to educational programs through which they hoped to gain a more sophisticated awareness of the world around them. Club members typically formed themselves into committees on labor, literature, art, drama, politics, education, and home. They prepared historical studies of general civic interest, which they read to each other. In addition to educating themselves, clubwomen organized working girls' societies, ran jail schools, and supported struggling girls' and women's schools and colleges.

By the end of the nineteenth century, woman's equal right to a formal education had largely been won, in principle if not in fact.[22] In addition to the state colleges that admitted women, several schools were established, such as Vassar (1861), Wellesley (1870), Smith (1875), and Bryn Mawr (1885), for women only. In opening their doors, these schools gave the few women economically privileged enough to enter them a significant new measure of moral and intellectual autonomy. Consciously and unconsciouly, these early women graduates pioneered in challenging their domestic vocational assignment in American family ideology. Jane Addams, Florence Kelley, and other early settlement house leaders, for example, dramatically demonstrated what social marvels women college graduates could achieve when they disregarded conventional conceptions of woman's duty.

THE MATERIAL FEMINIST TRADITION

Throughout the better part of the nineteenth century, a small number of thoughtful individuals in Europe and the United States became convinced that a collectively revised architecture would be crucial to the social empowerment of women. Adherents of that view and its practitioners have been described by Dolores Hayden as "material feminists" to indicate their conviction that the exploitation of women's domestic labor was central to the perpetuation of sexual inequality. They consistently proposed material solutions involving both economic and spatial change.[23] The two most influential material feminists were Welshman Robert Owen (1771–1858) and Frenchman Charles Fourier (1772–1837), both communitarian socialists whose ideas inspired dozens of residential experiments in the United States.

With an emphasis on providing quality child care to the children of working mothers, Owen published designs for groups of families, starting about 1813, which included collective nurseries, dining rooms, and kitchens. With the help of an architect in 1825, he developed a model for multifamily housing with community facilities that was both grand and provocative.

Fourier's rendition of socialized architecture, which he called a "phalanstery" or "unitary dwelling," paralleled Owen's both in its scale and in its blend of private and communal facilities. Fourier and his followers taught that the isolated household was an unacceptable impediment to the achievement of female equality; they campaigned for its abolition. According to Hayden, Owen's work was the inspiration for about fifteen communal experiments in the United States, beginning in the 1820s, whereas some thirty associations (or phalanxes) were built in the United States, starting in the 1840s. [24]

Through their American followers, Owen and Fourier exerted an

"Does a Man Support His Wife?" Anonymous cartoon published in 1911 by the Charlton Company as the frontispiece to a pamphlet containing essays by Gilman and British feminist Emmeline Pethick Lawrence. Lampooning popular notions of dependent, nonworking women at home, the tract debated subtleties in the economic relationship between husband and wife.

important influence on a large number of noncommunitarians as well. Catharine Beecher and Harriet Beecher Stowe, for example, despite their general enthusiasm for the detached, single-family household, did acknowledge that not every family was able to afford such an ideal dwelling. Although they devoted most of their attention to the organization of life within the isolated, single-family home, the Beecher sisters did occasionally discuss the advantages of "combined labor" in "Model Christian Neighborhoods" of ten to twelve families sharing a common cooked food service and laundry.

Just one generation later, Melusina ("Zina") Fay Peirce, a housewife from Cambridge, Massachusetts, was straightforwardly advocating domestic combination as the centerpiece of her political strategy. She urged women to form associations of twelve to fifty united households through which they could pool their homemaking skills for sale in the marketplace. Doing so would permit them to enjoy each other's company while achieving a new kind of woman-controlled economic power.

On May 6, 1869, Peirce presided over the first meeting of the Cambridge Cooperative Housekeeping Society in the home of her parents-in-law on Quincy Street. Shortly thereafter, several dozen Cambridge women, backed by committees of sympathetic men, began running a well-equipped neighborhood workplace on Bow Street in which they baked pies, washed clothes, and mended garments to be exchanged for cash on delivery. In spite of an impressively well developed theory and a wide circle of influential supporters, the housekeeping service lasted less than two years, undermined by husbands' animosity and a shortage of patronage.[25]

About the middle of the nineteenth century, the urban apartment hotel had become recognized as a built form with enormous potential for socializing domestic industries. Shortly before his death in 1838, Fourier himself had called attention to the progressive possibilites of apartment buildings in Paris. In the late 1850s, anarchist philosopher Stephen Pearl Andrews and twenty of his followers established a "Unitary Household" on Stuyvesant Street in New York City which combined private and shared communal spaces; it was so popular that it relocated to East Fourteenth Street in less than one year in order to accommodate about sixty more residents. Hayden describes Andrews's household as "a forerunner of the many urban apartment hotels built in the last quarter of the nineteenth century."[26]

Architect Philip G. Hubert's cooperatively owned apartment hotels, called Hubert Home Clubs, exemplified this communitarian model of urban dwelling; at least eight of them were built in New York City in the 1880s. During the same decade, Marie Stevens Howland was not only popularizing the architectural ideas of Charles Fourier in the United States but also helping to design the first plan for a complete city of kitchenless houses and apartment hotels; she and a civil engineer named Albert Owen worked for many years to build just such a city in Topolobampo, Mexico.[27]

Throughout the last half of the nineteenth century, the radical (and even the mainstream) press consistently carried lengthy discussions of communal housekeeping schemes and experiments. In 1868, for example, Elizabeth Cady Stanton's suffrage newspaper, *The Revolution,* carried an article by Harriet Beecher Stowe entitled "A Model Village." There Stowe portrayed an ideal cityscape complete with a town laundry, a town bakery, and a town cook shop "where soups and meats may be bought, ready for the table."[28] From November 1868 until March 1869, Zina Peirce published five articles in *Atlantic Monthly* entitled "Cooperative Housekeeping." In 1870 and 1871, Victoria Woodhull and her sister Tennessee Claflin ran a series of articles in their newspaper, *Woodhull and Claflin's Weekly,* about urban apartment hotels with cooperative child-care facilities. Hayden reports that as editor of the Boston suffrage paper, *Woman's Journal,* Mary Livermore gave very thorough coverage for many years to the subject of cooperative housekeeping; her paper even ran articles advocating male involvement in child care and housework.[29]

During the last fifteen years of the nineteenth century, many women in two new professional fields, social work and home economics, gave serious attention to the promise of collective housekeeping. In 1890 Ellen Swallow Richards and Mary Hinman Abel, two pioneering home economists, opened the first public kitchen in Boston, Massachusetts, to demonstrate how the latest household technology could be put to use in any neighborhood to prepare nutritious, inexpensive meals for working people. Having learned of the model public kitchen after its exhibition at the 1893 World's Columbian Exposition in Chicago, hundreds of social workers took note and copied the New England Kitchen throughout the United States.

The settlement house can be seen as an architectural innovation in the material feminist tradition, typically encompassing such urban facilities for working-class and professional women as central kitchens and dining rooms, child-care services, laundries, peer support groups, and evening classes. Hayden notes that there were more than 400 settlement houses in the United States by 1911, arguing that their provision of supportive physical and social spaces for women pursuing careers was an achievement quite as impressive as their community services offered to working-class families.[30]

Perhaps the most lively conversations about socializing housework were sparked by utopian novels depicting futuristic cities with centralized services. One hundred years ago, popular novels accounted for a much greater proportion of society's total entertainment than they do today in the television age. Utopian fiction by Marie Howland, William Dean Howells, Abby Morton Diaz, Bradford Peck, and Lois Waisbrooker, among many others, thus became the occasion for widespread consideration of value questions concerned with what the future environment would look like. Another material feminist vision was set forth by Henry Olerich; his *Cityless and Countryless World: An Outline of Practical Cooperative Individualism* portrayed collective kitchens, dining rooms, day-care, and recreation facilities in an egalitarian, genderless society located on the feminist planet Mars.[31]

Looking Backward by Edward Bellamy had the most phenomenal impact of these literary works; first published in 1888, it launched a major middle-class socialist movement. The Bellamy movement came to be called "Nationalism" because it advocated government ownership of all the means of production. As an important feature of state capitalism, Nationalists believed both that women should work outside the home and that the state should provide domestic services such as public restaurants, laundries, nurseries, and day schools to enable them to do so. In November 1890 there were 158 flourishing Nationalist clubs in twenty-seven states, sixty-eight of which were in California, sixteen of which were in New York City. California was especially congenial to Bellamy socialism; by October 1889 five Nationalist newspapers were being published there. Buhle notes that Boston was another Nationalist stronghold.[32]

In *Looking Backward,* Julian West, a young, well-to-do gentleman, falls into a deep, hypnotically induced sleep in the year 1887. When he awakens 113 years later, without having aged at all, the urban landscape around him has been completely transformed. The story consists of Mr. West's untiring inquiries of a kindly Dr. Leete and his daughter Edith as to how the Boston of yesteryear, with its extremes of wealth and poverty and its segregation of middle-class women in the home, has become an egalitarian commonwealth. In the new Boston, all women and men work for twenty-four years, starting at age twenty-one and ending at age forty-five, earning labor credit from the state. Oddly enough the biggest change of all turns out to be ideological since a hearty, familylike, "public spirit" has replaced the primary source of earlier evil, which was "excessive individualism." In the latter day, everyone is securely linked to everyone else, not just in word but in daily deed, in "the brotherhood of man."[33]

REVISITING THE OPTIMISM OF THE PROGRESSIVE ERA

The popularity of utopian novels toward the end of the nineteenth century had a much deeper root than their predating of television and radio. They expressed a spirit of hopefulness so immense as to make a contemporary reader scratch her head in disbelief. Given the negligible imitational impact of earlier communitarian experiments, why did these writers think that their ideas would make greater waves? What were their sources of inspiration? Why were they so optimistic?

It would be impossible to overstate the dramatic character of the shift in dominant world view between the beginning and the end of the nineteenth century. As the discoveries of Charles Darwin filtered into popular consciousness, the magnitude of the changed outlook left almost no one untouched. One result of the dawning awareness of evolutionary history was the enhancement of the prestige of the physical sciences. In every field, from cultural anthropology to biblical studies, the example of biological science had established the necessity of open-mindedness and painstaking fact finding in the pursuit of reliable knowledge. To enhance their projects in the public imagination, reformers looked to the "scientific" work of scholars as the secure foundation on which they proposed to build.

The surprising new sense that the earth had been around for billions and not merely thousands of years contributed to an elongation of historical sensibilites. The most intriguing relationships for many intellectuals became those between primitive forms of life, such as protozoa, and human beings, rather than those between generations of human beings themselves. The telescoping of ancient origins resulted in a tendency to romanticize the historical process itself. Stated most influentially by Herbert Spencer, the progression of life from one-celled to highly complex creatures came to be taken as incontrovertible evidence for a progressive reading of history. Because evolution has moved invariably in one direction, from simple to compound, lower to higher, went the reasoning, and because society can be interpreted as growing in accordance with the same laws, human history should appropriately be read as unilinear: Rightly understood, humanity is moving only a progressive direction.

In addition to the influence of Spencer's evolutionism, there were other streams feeding the optimistic spirit of turn-of-the-century reformers. Many read the Industrial Revolution, shifting production from household to factory, as the pattern that the remaining domestic industries (cooking, cleaning, child care, etc.) would reliably follow; like evolution itself, they believed that the progressive development of the home could not be stopped. They took hope as well from the number of voices being raised to protest the exploitation of the working classes. Recent advances in the technology of print media, as well as ongoing improvements in communication and travel, evoked the possibility that hearts once cold and ignorant could now be educated and ignited. Furthermore, although women were still disenfranchised, a few of them were inspiringly demonstrating their equal humanity by going to college and excelling in several professions. Showing its proclivity for expecting the best, the progressive imagination raced ahead to celebrate the positive influence that women would exert on politics, once they had the vote, and on the world at large, once they were the social and economic equals of men.

There is an enormous credibility gap between the end of the nineteenth century and the end of the twentieth. To our forebears, the beginning of a fresh new century augured well for the implementation of insights gained from the scientific way of thinking. Given the dropping and stockpiling of atomic bombs and other twentieth-century irrationalities, our outlook on the coming centennial can in no way be as euphoric as theirs. Whereas they could imagine that one day all would be well, we can too easily imagine that one day there will be no life on earth at all.

But despair is not the only lesson of the twentieth century. Having rediscovered crucial historical and psychological connections between generations of human beings, we can now learn a great deal from the naiveté as well as the insight, the failures as well as the successes of our foremothers and forefathers. Although we can no longer believe that forward is the only way human history is going, we can be instructed (and comforted) as we go by the recollection and companionship of an engaging feminist pioneer.

· CHAPTER TWO ·

Who Was Charlotte Perkins Gilman?

O Lord, take me out of this!
I do not fit!
My body does not suit my mind,
My brain is weak in the knees and blind,
My clothes are not what I want to find—
Not one bit!

My house is not the house I like—
Not one bit!
My church is built so loose and thin
That ten fall out where one falls in;
My creed is buttoned with a pin—
It does not fit!

"A Misfit"
CHARLOTTE PERKINS STETSON

A FEMINIST/SOCIALIST WITH A MISSION

Charlotte Anna Perkins Stetson Gilman lived from 1860 until 1935.[1] Variously celebrated as a poet, a preacher, an iconoclast, and a theoretician, Gilman dedicated herself to the advancement of women and the cultivation of socialist consciousness in the United States and throughout the world.

Gilman was a moral theologian whose object was "the improvement of the human race." She championed women's rights and socialism as two aspects of the same ongoing social evolutionary "world process." She was a deeply religious woman whose mysticism nourished her and whose conception of religious action was profoundly ethical. Although she belonged officially to no church or denomination, she was a fervent believer in and preacher of progressive religion. Her early papers include extensive notes for Sunday school classes and sermons. She was a frequent guest preacher in liberal Protestant pulpits, most commonly Unitarian ones.

Gilman's advocacy of women's concerns strongly informed the best of her writing and thinking. Her feminism was widely cultural in its analyses and prescriptions. Organizationally, she was active in the women's club movement, assisting with the development and leadership of several clubs in California. She appeared on innumerable speaker's platforms for clubs throughout the United States and at several international meetings of clubwomen. She strongly supported the women's suffrage movement but did not make it her number one priority. She recalled in her autobiography how she "had worked for Equal Suffrage when opportunity offered, believing it to be reasonable and necessary, though by no means as important as some of its protagonists held."[2] She recognized that constitutional equality with men would not be sufficient to liberate women.

Gilman's role in the nonpartisan socialist movement was that of an intellectual leader. She preached and lectured in all but four of the United States, writing dozens of books in a variety of styles. She was certain that evolution was moving society inexorably in a collectivist direction; to help it along she urged people to cooperate with each other across class lines rather than, as the Marxists suggested, to prepare for class struggle. She believed that socialism could be achieved by means of persuasion, that her talks and lectures to clubs and other organizations were daily helping to establish a new economic democracy in the United States. Of one such talk she wrote, "I lectured on the Principles of Socialism so convincingly that they passed a resolution in favor of those principles and their gradual adoption."[3] She delighted in disarming people of their objection that socialism was an alien, atheistic doctrine.

Gilman's life began and ended in the context of strong religious commitment. She was the great-granddaughter of the Reverend Lyman Beecher, the great-niece of Harriet Beecher Stowe, Catharine Beecher, Isabella Beecher, and the Reverend Henry Ward Beecher. She was surrounded as a child by religious persons with highly moral sensibilities. Her lifelong inner dialogue and sense of unity with the "Divine Life Force" can be seen in her diaries and poetry. Just before she died she wrote: "I have no faintest belief in personal immortality—no interest in nor desire for it. My life is in Humanity and That goes on. My contentment is in God—and That goes on."[4]

The main published primary source for reconstructing Gilman's life is her autobiography, *The Living of Charlotte Perkins Gilman,* which she was beginning to write in 1925 with less than total enthusiasm. To her friend, sociologist Edward A. Ross, she confided in a letter, "I have started in a feeble way on my Autobiography, but it does not interest me as much as it ought to. My real interest is in ideas, as you know."[5]

The book Gilman thus half-heartedly produced, although fascinating, actually raises as many questions as it answers. Of it she wrote, "Like a few pictures out of a big book too hastily turned in a dim light, are these memories."[6] Much of the book consists of diary entries strung together and expanded upon, with dates rendered none too carefully, often incompletely. In her biography, Mary Hill illustrates several discrepancies between Gilman's immediate rendering of an event in her journal and her recollected autobiographical version of the same episode. Looking back on her life from the vantage point of her sixties, Gilman tended to dwell on certain negative experiences, according to Hill, and to speak only of the positive aspects of mothering. It is important to note as well that a large portion of the autobiography, whose writing stretched over many years, was likely set down "in the difficult months immediately following the death of her husband Houghton Gilman, and immediately before her own."[7]

Throughout her life, domestic ideology was extremely irksome to Charlotte Gilman. From childhood she had aimed to be socially active in public affairs. Although she loved children and they her, she could never imagine confining the expression of her talent to the circumference of a private home, as middle-class family ideals suggested she should. Writing to a close friend in 1883 from a summer governess placement in Maine, she joked about being neither orthodox feminine nor masculine. "The men folks fish and hunt, the women folks knit and crochet and chatter, and I (neuter you observe!) Write & Draw & Paint and make myself generally useful."[8]

Gilman's life work can aptly be seen as a multifaceted effort to demolish the cultural paradigm of two gender spheres. She proposed instead one integrated universe in which every individual was expected to perform meaningful, remunerative labor, with domestic work conducted outside the home as a large-scale business. Changing neighborhood architecture to support women's participation in a unified world was the most sustained, practical focus of Gilman's lifelong feminist, socialist campaign.

AN UNCONVENTIONAL YOUTH

Gilman was born on July 3, 1860, in Hartford, Connecticut, the third of four children born to Mary Fitch Westcott Perkins and Frederick Beecher Perkins. Her parents were also second cousins. Their first and fourth-born children died in infancy. Their second child, Thomas Adie, was Charlotte's companion through childhood. Charlotte was named for two of her father's aunts, Charlotte and Anna Perkins.

Although her extended family commanded substantial social prestige in Connecticut and Rhode Island, Gilman's own childhood was beset by considerable economic uncertainty. Because her father had left home permanently when she was two years old, the life of Gilman's immediate family had an almost vagabond character from as far back as she could remember.

Frequent lengthy visits to relatives and family friends compensated the young Gilman for her decidedly vagrant beginnings. In addition to providing hospitality, several aunts, uncles, and acquaintances offered the child rather extraordinary intellectual stimulation. Growing up in the bosom of the Beecher family, she decided at a tender age to dedicate herself to a life of "world improvement."

Gilman's father was the son of Lyman Beecher's daughter Mary. From the Beechers and their associates, Gilman learned to revere the life of the socially consecrated mind. In her extended family circle, abolition, women's rights, and economic equality were righteous causes deserving the most prodigious efforts. Besides her paternal grandmother, Mary

Perkins, Great-aunts Catharine, Isabella, and Harriet, in particular, were important role models for Gilman as a child.

Outside of their several dwellings, Gilman's formal education was not exceptional. In more than one location, Mrs. Perkins conducted elementary school at home for her daughter, her son, and a few other children. Gilman thought well of her mother's work as an educator, later recalling: "She taught us admirably; . . . she was a phenomenally good teacher for the very young." Looking back on her youth she noted that she and Thomas had had to make do with "bits of schooling" here and there, which they "never had time to finish anywhere." As far as she could calculate, her "total schooling covered four years, among seven different schools," ending when she was fifteen.[9]

As a youngster, Gilman learned to question the pieties of middle-class family life. She described her mother as "Delicate and beautiful, . . . musical and . . . 'spiritual minded' " but also "painfully thwarted" in her desire for love and fulfillment.[10] Gilman's personal circumstances diverged significantly from the norms of domestic ideology, causing her to regard their authority skeptically. Mary Hill neatly summarizes the situation of Charlotte's mother: "Most of the women Charlotte knew were affluent; Mary wasn't. Most were settled; Mary moved around a lot. Most had conventional marriages; Mary was a divorced mother. Most enjoyed rather refined and leisured lives with maids, tutors, and butlers, whereas Mary was mother, maid, and household manager, as well as the educator and often even the bread-winner for her family."[11] In addition to raising questions about traditional verities, Gilman's unsettled youth contributed to her lifelong vagueness about her own social class status.

Gilman's mother and father, in varying ways, pressured their daughter to excel in intellectual pursuits. Frederick Perkins was a distinguished librarian whose career included the administration of both the Boston and the San Francisco public libraries. Exactly why he had moved away was always a painful mystery to Gilman. Proud of his scholarly achievements and clinging to the book lists he sent to her, she learned at a young age that her only route to intimacy with her father was a scholarly one.

The training Gilman received from her mother complemented the long-distance regimen of her father. Mary Westcott Perkins was deeply humiliated by the disappearance of her husband. In addition to her emotional loss, Fred's departure left her without a reliable source of income. To survive, she turned to friends and relatives for shelter and support. With her children, Mrs. Perkins became itinerant, transplanting her little family (according to Gilman's recollection) nineteen times in eighteen years, more often than not from one city to another. The three of them were frequent passengers on the Hartford-to-Springfield railroad until they finally settled more permanently in Providence, Rhode Island, when Gilman was thirteen years old.

While Mr. Perkins, by remote control, was teaching Gilman the supreme value of intellectual life, Mrs. Perkins was instructing her, day by day, in the dangers of the emotional life. To discourage her from becoming dependent on the affections of others, Gilman's mother was sternly undemonstrative with the little girl and very strict. For their different reasons and in their distinct ways, both Gilman's parents consistently rewarded her for being studious and independent.

There were four hiding places in Gilman's life where she could protect and nourish her affective life. In her athletic activities, her art, her spirituality, and her close friendships she could give expression to her moods, her vulnerabilities, and her emotional needs as well as her lively intelligence.

From youth to old age, Gilman paid regular attention to her personal health. She had a superb physique. She traced her commitment to fitness to a lecture on hygiene she had heard as a youth given by a woman physician named Dr. Studley. She "forthwith" took to " 'dress reform,' fresh air, cold baths, every kind of attainable physical exercise." She successfully campaigned for the establishment of the first gymnasium for women in Providence. She exulted in a strenuous program of athletic activity, savoring each new feat added to her repertoire. She was conscientious about eating properly and moderately. At forty-two, she joined a women's basketball team at Barnard College. The result of her rigorous training, she wrote, was "a cheerful vigor that enjoyed walking about five miles a day, with working hours from six A.M. to ten P.M. except for meals." In her sixties she confessed, "I never was vain of my looks, nor of any professional achievements, but am absurdly vain of my physical strength and agility."[12]

Gilman was a poet and a painter. She started to paint as a child, inspired by Aunt Harriet Stowe's watercolors of the ferns and flowers in the back yard. Her earliest diaries contain charming designs, sketches, and doodles, picturing people, dragons, beasts, and flowers. As a young woman she determined to attend the newly opened Rhode Island School of Design (RISD) despite her mother's objections. A family friend, Mrs. C. C. Smith of Boston, having recognized Gilman's talent, helped convince

Mrs. Perkins of the wisdom of cultivating it. After Mr. Perkins agreed to pay for it, Gilman became a student at RISD, later reporting that she had "learned much" there.

After art school, Gilman had some ambition to work as a political cartoonist. Graphic art, to her, was more than an avenue of satisfying self-expression. It also represented several ways in which she could earn a living. To augment her income at various times in her life, she put her brushes and sketching pencils to work, sometimes giving art lessons, at other times painting advertising cards for businesses.

In addition to painting and drawing, Gilman wrote a lot of poetry. She showed an affinity for rhyme, meter, and flowing cadences as a youngster, reporting the practice of rendering her lessons for "history, grammar, and once even arithmetic class in rhyme."[13] She wrote many verses in which she poured out her intense affection for special friends. Sometimes she set a diary entry in rhyme, thereby transforming an everyday event into a memorable occasion. The poetry of certain writers popular during her childhood delighted her, inspiring her to memorize "miles of it" while combing her hair.

Gilman used her flair for poeticizing to heighten the effect of her teachings about evolution, women, and social consciousness. In addition, much of her poetry was not pedagogical at all but rather a record of her most profound inner struggles for sanity and strength. Writing poetry was frequently a means of therapeutic release for her, part of her process of working through a personal crisis or weighty decision.

Gilman was on familiar terms with the Deity. A lively spirituality was an important dimension in her sense of self. She fashioned an eclectic system of religious belief, one that was nonsectarian, rationalist, and in many details similar to Unitarianism. She had a dynamic, transformatory conception of the divine. To her, God was the "Life Force," initiating and sustaining the processes of evolution, inviting persons to cooperate in the divine agenda of social improvement. She was convinced that "this religion of mine underlies all my Living, is the most essential part of my life."[14]

As a young woman, Gilman set out to build and to live by "a reliable religion founded on fact." She was a firm believer in intelligent religion. She had no investment in inherited doctrine, a bias against dogma per se, "an innate incredulity."[15] Her approach to theology was inquisitive and experiential. Her feminism introduced a critical principle into her metaphysics. She often denounced the arrogance that falsely ascribed maleness to the deity. "God is not a male progenitor," she insisted.[16] She consistently urged women to use their brains as well as their knee joints in the service of social religion.

Gilman drew both strength and solace from her personal mysticism. She was deeply convinced that she was a vital part of the "Living God," that divine energy was available to and expressing itself through her. Religion for her was the ground upon which rationality and emotion met and embraced each other. Two verses of one of her poems, entitled "The Living God," illustrate the fervent quality of her mysticism.

> Not near enough! Not clear enough!
> O God, come nearer still!
> I long for thee! Be strong for me!
> Teach me to know thy will!
>
> Ah, clear as light! As near! As bright!
> O God! My God! My own!
> Command thou me! I stand for thee!
> And I do not stand alone![17]

Gilman approached the natural world sacramentally, finding great satisfaction and peace through her communion with the out-of-doors, most especially in California.

Although it strengthened and comforted her, Gilman had built a religion on a highly selective reading of "fact." Had she not pushed the question of evil totally out of her purview, her religion would have been much more "reliable." As she saw it, the Life Force to which she related was glorious, all-powerful, perfectly just, immanent within the processes of evolution, and accessible to her. While frequently turning to "God" in her own pain, she was oblivious to contradictions between notions of divine justice and divine omnipotence. Her pretense that evil in the world was merely ephemeral seriously weakened both her personal faith and her natural theology.

Close friendships formed the fourth sanctuary for Gilman's emotional life. According to the testimony of friends, she had a lively sense of humor, which contributed importantly to her zest for life. She laughed a lot, especially at herself. She often played comic roles in dramatic productions since she did not mind making a fool of herself; in fact, she confided, she greatly enjoyed it. She had a beautiful smile.

Related by both kinship and friendship to a wide circle of prominent New England families such as the Hales and the Hazards, Gilman had numerous friends who were male. She prided herself on having been a

Middle-aged Gilman, at leisure.

"tomboy" as a girl. Growing up, she and her brother had goaded each other into continuous mischievous escapades, culminating in a contest to see who could most accurately spit on the bald head of a man passing underneath them on the stairwell of their apartment building. The sons of several families in Cambridge and Providence were Gilman's frequent teenaged companions.

At every age, Gilman found special comfort in the camaraderie of her female friends. She described some of her most memorable attachments with glowing ardor. She recalled, for example, her "devoted affection" for Etta Talcott, a "pale, long-haired" schoolmate, and Harriet White, her heart's "second devout affection." From young womanhood until literally the day she died, Gilman depended very substantially on Grace Ellery Channing Stetson, her "more than sister." She paid homage to the memory of May Diman, "the most utterly charming," for whom she wrote many love poems, and to handsome Helen Hazard for whom she had begun a valentine verse, "Fair one, whom I adore!" By no means running out of superlatives, Gilman characterized Martha Luther as "immeasurably the dearest" of her girlhood friends. The two had formed their bond when Martha was sixteen and Gilman seventeen years old. Gilman wrote of it, "We were not only extremely fond of each other, but we had fun together, deliciously." When Martha married a Mr. Lane and moved away from Providence, she left a deeply disconsolate Gilman. "Losing Martha" was a terrible blow to the older girl.

Although the effects of her parents' sternly cerebral expectations were mitigated by her fitness programs, her art, her spirituality, and her friendships, Gilman later considered herself to have been a very austere young woman. Never satisfied with herself as a youth, she invented an arduous program of character building and study designed to promote progressive perfection.[18] Optimistic about her capacity to change the world almost single-handedly, she consistently set herself up to be a disappointment to herself. Arriving at adulthood, Gilman expected great feats of moral heroism from members of her generation, particularly its women.

MARRIAGE, MOTHERHOOD, AND MELANCHOLIA: WALTER, KATHARINE, AND DIVORCE

While she was twenty-one, Gilman met a handsome young painter in Providence named Charles Walter Stetson. After a brief acquaintance, he asked her to marry him. There then ensued a "terrible two years" of uncertainty in which Gilman could not decide if she wanted to marry him. Terrified that she would lose her potential for public service once she had wed, she was tormented by her rational conviction that "a woman should be able to have marriage and motherhood, and do her work in the world also."[19] Convinced that she as much as a man had the right both to "intimate personal happiness" and to "complete devotion" to her work, she could not attain a satisfying assurance concerning the "right" thing for her to do. The "philosophic steam-engine" (as she referred to herself) had been brought to a standstill.

In May 1884, having grown tired of saying no, Gilman was married to Mr. Stetson in Providence by Stetson's father, a Baptist minister.[20] The young bride became pregnant within two months and gave birth to Katharine Beecher Stetson, on March 23, 1885. During the nine months she was carrying the baby, she had experienced periods of seriously debilitating depression, a condition she and Stetson expected to subside after the baby's arrival. But it was not to be so. Instead, it got worse. Despite her determination to rise above her personal misery, to be a good wife and a good mother, she could not escape the fact that she had become a "mental wreck."

Before resorting to divorce, Gilman made two major attempts to regain her health and composure. One involved travel and reunion with friends in California, far from her domestic responsibilites. The other entailed putting herself in the "care" of a prominent neurologist, Dr. S. Weir Mitchell of Philadelphia, a specialist in the treatment of so-called neurasthenic (hysterical) women.

Being on the Pacific Coast for the fall and winter did Gilman a world of good. In fact, the very act of getting away itself was a tonic. She reported, "from the moment the wheels began to turn, the train to move, I felt better."[21] Surrounded by the warmth both of southern California's exotic out-of-doors and of the Channing family's affectionate attentions, Gilman recovered her sense of well-being. But it did not last for long. The aura of healthiness had begun to fade before her arrival back home; she caught a heavy bronchial cold on the two-week train trip. To her great chagrin, she found that "within a month I was as low as before leaving. . . . Soon ensued the same utter prostration, the unbearable inner misery, the ceaseless tears."[22]

After coming to grips with the fact that it was something about being at home that made her sick, Gilman took her second major step in search of restoration. After writing Weir Mitchell a long letter in advance, detailing the history of her illness, Gilman set out for Philadelphia to partake of the famous physician's "rest cure." But her hopefulness concerning the doctor's curative powers proved to be unwarranted.

From a modern perspective, the misogyny in Weir Mitchell's approach to women's health was blatant. Among his other patients were Jane Addams a few years ahead of Gilman and Edith Wharton a few years after. He disapproved of intellectual activity on the part of women and classified it as pathological. Upon her arrival he told Gilman, scornfully, that he had already treated two "Beecher women." Convinced that their illnesses had been exacerbated by their stubborn, unnatural imitation of men, he suspected his new patient of similar tendencies.

Mitchell's rest cure consisted of putting the patient to bed and keeping her there, the intention being so to infantilize the sick person as to make her totally dependent upon the doctor. When her time was up, Mitchell sent Gilman home with the following orders: "Live as domestic a life as possible. Have your child with you all the time. . . . Lie down an hour after each meal. Have but two hours' intellectual life a day. And never touch pen, brush or pencil as long as you live."[23]

After several months of following his directions "rigidly," Gilman realized that her condition had actually deteriorated, that she was more helpless than she had been before going to Philadelphia. Summoning her dormant decisiveness, Gilman rejected Mitchell's system and began to take charge of her life once again. By the fall of 1887, she and Stetson had decided to separate before divorcing. Walter moved back to his studio as a first step. About one year later, after dismantling their home and consolidating her resources, Gilman set out with Grace Channing for California where Gilman had decided to launch her professional life. They took three-year-old Katharine with them. In choosing divorce, Gilman took the only exit she could find out of the morass of inert melancholia.

WRITER AND PUBLIC SPEAKER: LAUNCHING A CAREER IN CALIFORNIA

Life in Pasadena again proved a tonic for Gilman's spirit. This time Dr. Channing, Grace's father, had arranged for Gilman and Katharine to rent a small cottage adjacent to the Channing home, which facilitated the sharing of meals, free time, and family concerns. Between 1888 and 1891, Grace Channing and Gilman began collaborating in the writing of plays.

At the same time, Gilman was establishing herself as an author in her own right. She started to write both to express her social ideas and to earn some income. Discovering that she could write very quickly, she developed the habit of dashing things off with little attention to editing, a practice she continued throughout her life. To illustrate her remarkably prolific literary output dating from the Pasadena days, she wrote, "In that first year of freedom I wrote some thirty-three short articles, and twenty-three poems, besides ten more child-verses."[24]

In September 1891, Gilman and Katharine, with the elder woman's special new friend, Adeline E. Knapp (known as Delle or Dora), moved to Oakland, California, where Gilman's ailing mother, Mary Perkins, joined them. The foursome moved to a second Oakland boardinghouse early in 1892, the very strenuous management of which Gilman assumed when the former manager left abruptly.

Caring for her cancer-ridden mother and several other sick boarders was very difficult for Gilman, especially when Katharine (Kate) came down with whooping cough. But despite the stress and the endless household responsibilities, she managed to maintain the flow of her writing. During the winter of 1893, one of her diary entries reports: "Have done about fifteen pieces of salable work this month—, three lectures, three poems, nine articles of one sort or another. Received $40.00 therefor so far. Fair work for an overworked invalid."[25] Mary Perkins died, with Gilman beside her, in early March 1893.

In April 1894, the Stetsons' divorce became final. Late that same year, shortly after Stetson had married Grace Channing, Gilman sent nine-year-old Katharine east to make her home with Mr. Stetson and his new wife.

In deciding to share her postdivorce parenting with Stetson, Gilman gave herself a longed-for opportunity to immerse herself completely in her civic career. She told herself and her little girl that it was going to be good—and fun—for Katharine to live with her father and stepmother in a more "normal" household.

But Gilman paid a very high price for this decision, in guilt, resentment, and public censure. At the time that Gilman sent Katharine east to him, Stetson was by no means clamoring to have his daughter come to stay with him. Newly wed, he would have preferred not to assume day-to-day responsibility for the child just then. But Gilman had "new work opening" for her in San Francisco in a place unsuitable for a child. So she "arranged" to have Katharine live with her father for a while.[26] In so doing she incurred the torment of her own conscience, some long-range resentment from the Stetsons, and the wrath of conservative Californians expressed most vehemently in the Hearst newspapers.

Gilman turned to her former husband and Grace Channing Stetson for help in part because there were neither affordable systems of quality child care nor reasonable housework support services available to her in Oakland. Since there were no such accommodations, Gilman had to choose between her world betterment campaign and her homemaking duties. As a single parent in a detached household, she could not sustain both the multiple responsibilites of head-of-family and those of Socratic improver of the race. Given the necessity of choice, she decided to favor her role as social reformer.

After Katharine moved east, Gilman needed consolation and company. She moved in with her journalist comrade and devoted friend, Helen (Weeks) Campbell, in San Francisco. Campbell, who was thirty years her senior, was an important mentor to Gilman, crusading for the rights of wage-earning women and helping to found the National Household Economics Association. Together the two women edited the *Impress,* which was the magazine of the Pacific Coast Women's Press Association (PCWPA). While they lived and worked together, the elder woman inspired Gilman with her fiery denunciations of capitalist offenses and comforted her, day by day, both with companionship and with the provision of delicious meals and other household services. Their collaboration was a significant one to Campbell as well, who thanked Gilman for her "deep interest" and cooperation in the introduction to *Household Economics,* citing in particular Gilman's poem "City's Beauty."[27]

One of Gilman's most passionate causes during her California years was Bellamy Nationalism. Thrilled by the seriousness attached by Bellamy to the advancement of women, she began writing for Nationalist publications and lecturing widely to Nationalist clubs in the late 1880s. Frances Willard, Mary Livermore, Gilman's uncle Edward Everett Hale, and William Dean Howells were among the enthusiastic recruits she was joining as a Bellamyite. Revering Bellamy as the "prophet who made us understand and believe," she found in the Nationalist movement both a congenial political milieu and her own personal "road to fame."[28] Her long poem, "Similar Cases," which draws an analogy between human and animal evolution and the absurdity of resistance to either, put Gilman on the socialist celebrity map in 1890, winning her widespread admiration and innumerable lecture invitations.[29]

Gilman's popularity as writer and lecturer was also expanding through her involvement with numerous women's clubs. After she moved to northern California, she served for a time as president of the PCWPA. About that time she made this list of the clubs to which she belonged:

> The P.C.W.P.A.
> The Ebell Society.
> The Woman's Alliance.
> The Economic Club.
> The Parents Association.
> The State Council of Women.

The following jottings from her diary at that time provide a glimpse of the energy she was devoting to club endeavors.

> W.P.A. [Women's Press Association], one afternoon a month, and two days more on an average; Ec. Club two afternoons and one evening; Ebell two evenings and two more to prepare; Pa. [Parents] Assn. two evenings; St. C. of W. [State Council of Women] one afternoon. . . . W.P.A., I am on Child Labor committee and also on education. I wish to ascertain and present information on these subjects. Try to keep up the general ideal. Ebell; furnish four more sociological papers. Ec. Club; Write papers, read, discuss, exhort, work. Pa. Assn., Organize and push the general society. Plan for the work at large. Visit local groups as desired. Make it go. St. Council, Help organize. Help push. A large, slow thing this. Should be a City council also.[30]

As she lectured in wider and wider circles and worked at the grass roots, Gilman demonstrated herself to be an indefatigable student of human progress and a very articulate cheerleader on its behalf.

Between the years 1895 and 1900, the circumference of Gilman's professional activity expanded from cross-country lecture circuits to trips abroad to attend international conferences, sometimes as featured speaker. During that period, she relished the experience of being "at large," as she put it, visiting Hull House, staying with friends and new acquaintances in the towns and cities she visited, going to women's congresses, suffrage meetings, and conventions of clubwomen. Having no address for a period of years (apart from that of her booking agent) had not only satisfied her taste for adventure; it had also established her sense of professional competence. Being so long on the move had exempted her from household maintenance long enough to establish a solid reputation for herself as a feminist teacher.

At the 1896 convention of the National American Woman's Suffrage Association (NAWSA), Gilman was the first person to speak against a resolution disavowing connection to Elizabeth Cady Stanton's *Women's Bible* project; she argued that the association should encourage rather than repudiate scholarly feminist projects like Stanton's, lest the woman suffrage, when attained, be in vain. The resolution of censure passed nonetheless, by a vote of 53–41; among those voting with the majority were two future presidents of NAWSA, Carrie Chapman Catt and the Reverend Anna Howard Shaw.[31]

While attending the International Socialist and Labor Congress in London in 1896 as a delegate from the California Federation of Trades, Gilman made friends with some English admirers of Bellamy, including Beatrice and Sidney Webb and George Bernard Shaw; she was so appreciative of their educational campaign promoting the nationalization of industries that she joined their Fabian Society and wrote for the *American Fabian* when she returned to the United States.

In addition to her socialist and women's club ties, Gilman was strongly connected to academic sociology. Of all her associates, none was more important to her than Lester Frank Ward of Washington, D.C. (later of Brown University), and Edward A. Ross of the University of Wisconsin. Professors Ward and Ross were academic innovators, helping to establish sociology as an independent field of study. Both of them were anxious to bring the findings of their new discipline to bear on the burning social issues of the day.

In an important dimension of their reformist sociology, both Ward and Ross took the "woman question" very seriously. They appreciated Gilman's charismatic authority as an articulate, assertive woman, admiring her witty, iconoclastic style. They entertained her when her travels brought her near them, wrote her letters of encouragement, and persuaded her on several occasions to collaborate with them in writing projects as well as on panel discussions.

Gilman's partnership with Professors Ward and Ross gave her a sense of belonging to an elite fraternity of vanguard intellectuals, leading the way to a socialist, nonsexist world. Their colleagueship was both exciting and flattering. She reveled in talking with them about books, ideas, principles, and policies. Since they were learned like her father, their attentions filled her need for validation and scholarly companionship. They respected her intense ambition to be inclusive, to relate everything to everything else in a systematic social theory. They encouraged her to believe that creating a comprehensive moral system, established on the foundation of scientific sociology and expressed in plain language, was the most important work she could undertake. They applauded her polemical fire, her seriousness about the vocation of writing, and her deft versatility with words. She was proudly their associate and they her coworkers.

Following the publication of "Similar Cases," Gilman's next three major publishing achievements involved a short story, a book of poems, and her first theoretical book about sexism, *Women and Economics.* The short story, entitled "The Yellow Wallpaper," was first published in the *New England Magazine* of 1892. Later anthologized by William Dean Howells as an outstanding American short story, "The Yellow Wallpaper" was Gilman's creative way of retaliating against Weir Mitchell for his abuse of her. She wrote it, she said, to convince the doctor "of the error of his ways" and thereby "to save people from being driven crazy." Learning many years later from close friends of Mitchell that "he had altered his treatment of neurasthenia since reading "The Yellow Wallpaper," she exulted, "If that is a fact, I have not lived in vain."[32]

Gilman wrote verses for all the causes in which she believed in addition to poetry of love, nature, and spiritual struggle. While living in the San Francisco area, she became close friends and political comrades with many other writers and poets, including Edwin Markham and Hamlin Garland. Two of her "Socialist friends" in Oakland published a small collection of seventy-five of her poems, *In This Our World,* in 1893. The same collection was published in England in 1895 and in Boston in 1898; an enlarged edition was published in Boston in 1908. Among the most avid fans of Gilman's poetry were numerous Unitarian clergy who used it widely in their sermons.[33]

Gilman had been writing essays, sermons, and speeches on ethical aspects of social life for almost ten years when she decided to write a book about the "Economic Relation of the Sexes" in 1897. She drafted the work, which was eventually titled *Women and Economics,* "in seventeen days, in five different houses," while visiting several friends around New England.[34] Published first in 1898, *Women and Economics* is a treatise, in fifteen chapters, on the injustice and adverse consequences to both women and society of women's financial dependence upon men. In her book, Gilman argued that the relatively primitive state of the human female's individual development was due to the atrophy of her productive ("self preservational") faculties and the exaggeration of her distinctive sexual features. The segregation of woman to the unspecialized sphere of family life, she insisted, required a highly unnatural constriction in the

exercise of her human capacities. She called for the widespread development of collective domestic facilities to allow women to break out of their
household detainment and find their place in a nonsegregated world of
esteemed work. *Women and Economics* was widely read in the United States
and abroad, so much so that it was reprinted in seven editions and
translated into seven languages.

WIFE AGAIN: HOUGHTON, CAREER, FULFILLMENT, AND DISILLUSIONMENT

In March 1897 Gilman looked up a favorite cousin of hers, George
Houghton Gilman, whom she had not seen for fifteen years. Houghton, as
he was known, was a Wall Street lawyer, seven years her junior, whose
mother was her father's sister. As youngsters, they had corrresponded
affectionately on matters of childhood concern. As their friendship deep-
ened, it took a romantic turn. They were married on June 11, 1900, in
Detroit, Michigan. A sympathetic Unitarian cleric performed the ceremony after an Episcopalian had refused to do so on account of Charlotte
Gilman's divorce.

On their honeymoon, the Gilmans stayed briefly in Detroit and
Toronto and then took a boat trip down Lake Champlain to a large resort
hotel. From the earliest days of their marriage, Houghton encouraged his
wife to continue her writing and lecturing. Having assisted her with
editing before they were married, he continued to provide a sympathetic
ear after the wedding, consistently extending very substantial help to her.
While traveling alone, Gilman's daily letters addressed to "My own Best-
Loved" reveal that her relationship with Houghton afforded her not only
profound comfort and stability but also a great deal of joy. Her affectionate
name for him was "Ho"; his for her was "Chopkins." They were married
for thirty-four years, twenty-two of which they lived in New York City.
During this period, her daughter Katharine alternated visits with the
Stetsons and the Gilmans, making her home with the Gilmans on a regular
basis. In 1922 the Gilmans moved into the spacious wing of a stately
Gilman family home on Washington Street in Norwich Town, Connecticut; Mr. Gilman's brother and his wife were living in the main part of the
house at the time.

In addition to her ongoing writing and lecture tours throughout the
United States, Gilman continued to make occasional trips abroad after her
second marriage. In 1904 she attended the International Congress of

Eight-year-old Katharine Beecher Stetson with her mother, in October 1893, in Oakland, California. Labeled "Our Kate."

Women in Berlin. She went on an extensive European trip in 1905, with speaking engagements in England, Holland, Germany, Austria, and Hungary. In 1913 she took part in the International Woman Suffrage Congress in Budapest. In the early years of the new century, her articles were a familiar feature in the Sunday magazines of major newspapers. She belonged to the New York chapter of the Women's Trade Union League and was a frequent contributor to its magazine, *Life and Labor.*

In September 1905 Gilman added her voice to those of William English Walling, Upton Sinclair, Thomas Wentworth Higginson, Clarence Darrow, Jack London, and several others who wanted to cultivate college students and graduates for the socialist cause. They founded the Intercollegiate Socialist Society (ISS), which produced a magazine called the *Intercollegiate Socialist* and by 1915 had sixty chapters in colleges and universities. Following the First World War, the ISS changed its name to the League for Industrial Democracy, which had a youth organization called Students for a Democratic Society.[35]

Throughout her public career, Gilman's simultaneous advocacy of socialist reorganization and women's emancipation made her a misfit in both the socialist and the women's movements. While applauding the brilliance of her denunciations of privatism, greed, and imperialism, leaders of the Socialist party were terribly suspicious of the directness with which she approached gender concerns. To function comfortably within the party, she would have had to mute her feminist analysis on behalf of a more orthodox class approach. She was unwilling to do this.

Likewise, Gilman's attacks on the organization of family and economic life under monopoly capitalism were too radical for the mainstream of the women's movement. As NAWSA narrowed its focus from its earlier, cultural feminism to single-minded pursuit of the vote, her recurrent assaults on male egoism in all its forms became an acute embarrassment. Suffragists had chosen a conservative strategy, which insisted that votes for women would change nothing at all save for a general elevation of moral tone throughout the land. In advocating "kitchenless homes" and public ownership of the means of production, Gilman placed herself at odds with a majority of suffragists. Although she joined and helped to found a number of progressive associations, she did not have a central, long-term political base.

Gilman's organizational homelessness made her a free-lance radical, working on the boundaries between the two movements. As she saw it, her task was to educate both sides as to their unity of purpose. She believed that the equality of women would be achieved at the same time that collectivism was established. She saw the socialization of domestic industries and the full human development of women as complementary aspects of one evolutionary process. Economically independent women were just as essential to the realization of socialism, she insisted, as socialized homes were to the emancipation of women. In an oft-published poem, Gilman asserted this socialist-feminist unity in rhyme.

> "A lifted world lifts women up,"
>   The Socialist explained.
>   "You cannot lift the world at all
>   While half of it is kept so small,"
>   The Suffragist maintained.
>
> The world awoke, and tartly spoke:
>   "Your work is all the same;
>   Work together or work apart,
>   Work, each of you, with all your heart—
>   Just get into the game![36]

Suggesting that economic injustice was a somewhat more pernicious evil than gender injustice, Gilman wrote that "Socialism by removing poverty removes the largest temptation on earth; and by ensuring the economic freedom of women, removes the next largest."[37] Insisting that the two causes were indispensable to each other, she confidently expected to see the progressive emancipation of women in a gradually collectivizing society as the twentieth century unfolded.

In the fall of 1909, Gilman launched the most astonishing project of her life, a monthly magazine which she entitled *The Forerunner.* In her fiftieth year she decided she needed a reliable medium of expression for her particular blend of socialism and feminism. When asked why she was not satisfied writing for existing periodicals such as *Life and Labor* and the *Woman's Journal,* she replied, "Why did not John Wesley preach in the established church?"[38] Tired of having her manuscripts rejected, she wanted a secure agency for proselytizing, a regular lobby for her composite agitation.

Published every month from November 1909 until December 1916, the *Forerunner* is an exuberant expression of literary creativity and moral passion, a colorful demonstration of Gilman's extraordinary stamina. Not only did she own and edit the magazine; she wrote every word of each thirty-page issue in its entirety. For one dollar a year, subscribers could count on receiving, each month, a short story, several poems, articles, book reviews, a chapter of a serialized novel, and a chapter of a provocative work of nonfiction. During the first year, the magazine had a cover illustration and advertisements for such items as Fels-Naptha soap and Moore's fountain pens. (She ran ads that year only for products she could personally recommend.) Katharine Stetson, Gilman's daughter, drew the picture that graced the cover of the first fourteen issues. Her drawing portrays a woman and a man, of equal proportions, with arms interlocked, embracing between them both a small child and the globe upon which the child is standing. Gilman stated her hopes for the *Forerunner* as follows: "It is to stimulate thought; to arouse hope, courage and impatience; to offer practical suggestions and solutions, to voice the strong assurance of better living, here, now, in our own hands to make."[39]

Several women's clubs in New York City were an important part of Gilman's network during the *Forerunner* years. She was an early member of Heterodoxy, a luncheon club that met every other Saturday in Greenwich Village, starting in 1912. Founded and sustained by Unitarian clergywoman and political activist Marie Jenney Howe, Heterodoxy was a dynamic group of unconventional women, which included a surprising diversity of life styles, political views, and ages. Several well-known radicals, such as Henrietta Rodman, Crystal Eastman, Zona Gale, and Grace Nail Johnson, were among the original "Heterodites." The group continued to meet until the 1940s.

In addition to its regular Saturday noon programs in which members told each other about their lives and addressed topics of current interest, Heterodoxy sponsored educational programs for the general public. At one such meeting, both Houghton and Charlotte Gilman were among the prominent New Yorkers who gave speeches, each of them just five minutes in length, to answer the arguments of antisuffragists. At another Heterodoxy event, a "feminist mass meeting" held at Cooper Union, Charlotte Gilman was a featured guest, speaking on the topic "The Right to Specialize in Home Industries."[40]

Gilman took an emphatic stand in a split that occurred within Heterodoxy. Shortly after the United States entered the First World War in April 1917, the club's sisterly bonds had become severely strained by antagonisms between supporters of the war effort and pacifists. Gilman, a hawk, was one of the first to follow journalist Rheta Childe Dorr out of the club as a statement of both nationalist and antipacifist fervor. Despite her consternation with opponents of the war, Gilman maintained close friend-ships with other club members, even after she moved to Connecticut. She was especially devoted to Marie Jenney Howe, whom she very much admired.

In April 1913 a group of women under the leadership of Alice Paul and Lucy Burns became impatient with the suffrage strategy of NAWSA. To escalate the Votes for Women campaign, they mobilized a spirited group, the Congressional Union, which functioned within NAWSA for about a year. Burns and Paul had caught fire during the time they spent working with the militant wing of the British Suffrage Movement in England. When the Union's differences with NAWSA intensified, it broke with the parent organization and renamed itself the National Woman's party. Gilman was on the National Advisory Council of the Woman's party from 1916 to 1920. She described the rationale and tactics of the party very succinctly in an article in the *Forerunner* of August 1916, entitled "The National Woman's Party."[41]

By the early 1920s, Gilman was having more doubts about the achievability of her socialist-feminist designs. As a sixty-year old, she was appalled by younger women's increasing preoccupation with sexual liber-ation, as they took advantage of newly available contraceptive devices. After the suffrage was won in 1918, most middle-class women were content to enjoy their new freedoms and relax about larger social con-cerns. Gilman objected to Freudianism since she believed Freud's exces-sive emphasis upon libidinal drives was dangerously distracting to new women citizens. Poking fun at the "Lust thou art to lust returnest" mentality, she was highly critical of recreational sex. She saw social evolution making it possible for women to achieve secure, creative eco-nomic independence; she begged them not to become further locked into their sexuality.[42]

The Gilman's move to Norwich Town, Connecticut, in 1922, had nativist connotations. Gilman expressed "measureless relief" upon leaving the "conglomerate races" flooding into New York City to take up resi-dence in a very homogeneous Anglo-Saxon community. She was never totally free of racist attitudes. One minor thread in her argument for the reorganization of domesticity concerned the ill effects of having ignorant servants around who were generally inferior to their employers. Like most progressive social scientists, she subscribed to anthropologist Lewis Henry Morgan's account of invariable evolutionary stages in racial development, stages he characterized as "Savagery, Barbarism, and Civilization." She

Houghton and Charlotte Gilman playing croquet beside their vegetable garden in Norwich Town, Connecticut, about 1930.

confidently assumed that the superior Nordic race had reached the highest known pinnacle of civilization. Aghast at the "rampant" quality of lower-class immigration into the United States, she was condescending toward "lesser" races.

Gilman considered "the negro race" to be "from a status far lower" than her own, a status which she characterized alternately as "Barbarism" or as "Savagery."[43] To combat the sexist assumption that woman's only reason for living was procreation, for example, she invoked a racist stereotype, commending an educated white woman for "serving the community better than the negress with her score of picaninnies."[44] Although she reported speaking to a colored women's club at their church in 1899,[45] there is no evidence that she established reciprocal relationships with women of color or that she listened seriously to the stories and concerns of black women. In her stories she did not hesitate to mock the dialect of ex-slaves or to tell jokes that insulted black people. The only women of color in her stories were domestic servants at whose expense she made sport. The racist message of her fiction was that black women did not exist except insofar as they served and amused white women.

Gilman did stand up unequivocally against racism on several occasions. At the 1903 convention of the National American Woman's Suffrage Association in New Orleans, for example, she was the only person who spoke out against the literacy requirement for the vote, a measure advocated by those who wanted to take advantage of antiblack, anti-immigrant feelings to gain the vote for white women.[46] At other times she chided her fellow white Americans for their enthnocentrism as well as their exploitation of other racial groups. "For any separate nationality to look down on another," she wrote, "shows 'provincialism,' and for us of the United States of America to look down on the nations from which we are constructed is palpably worse; not only wrong but ridiculous. . . . That we have cheated the Indian, oppressed the African, robbed the Mexican and childishly wasted our great resources is ground for shame."[47] She designated the four most urgent moral challenges facing Americans as (1) overcoming the injuries of slavery, (2) controlling immigration rationally, (3) including women in the definition of humanity and the conduct of society, and (4) achieving economic democracy.[48] In 1916 she expressed dismay at the lynching of a black man in Waco, Texas.[49] She frequently condemned anti-Semitism, calling it "the hideous injustice of Christianity to Jews."[50]

In spite of her protests, Gilman could not see the contradictions within her own position on the subject of race. Although she expressed disgust at the behavior of dominant groups toward minorities, she did not question her own sense of racial superiority. Nor did she have a satisfactory way of thinking about relationships between classes and racial or ethnic groups. As a result, her proposals for repairing the injuries of race were seriously flawed. Her scheme for "civilizing" former slaves by conscripting them into regiments for the learning of vocational skills, for example, was racist from its inception as "The Negro Problem." Her stated belief in the ultimate equality of all races boiled down to an expectation that other races would become more and more like hers. She saw the United States as a molding and not a melting pot. The policies she favored featured forced assimilation into the mold of so-called civilization. Social practices other than those received from northern European ancestors were considered "savage" or "barbaric" survivals, which had to be purged lest they retard the development of the more "civilized" host state.

Gilman's racism was part of a decidedly snobbish world view in which she presumed her words to have universal appeal. Showing her naive elitism, she took her own experience as normative for the whole human family. From her favored vantage point, she presumed to prescribe remedies for all the world's ills. Functioning as an exceptional woman on the fringes of white male academia, she assumed the role of expert on assorted social problems. With no stable constituency to challenge and inform her, she developed a disconnected arrogance about her ideas. "As I had planned the programs for those Congresses of Women," she wrote, "I planned programs for the world, seeing clearly the gradual steps by which we might advance to an assured health, a growing happiness. If they did not see it, would not do it, that was not my fault; my job, my one preeminent work, was to 'see' and to 'say,' and I did it."[51] Especially as intellectual system builder, Gilman sometimes succumbed to the view, not uncommon among Western Academics, that specially gifted minds should have a preeminent role in defining the social future.

Ironically, Gilman's voice reached the farthest when she was content to speak to middle-class women like herself. She knew and respected their circumstances. When she spoke out of her own experience as a woman crippled by social conventions, she voiced the yearnings of millions of women muted by isolation and humiliation. Her life and work illustrate a lesson learned in many political struggles since her time, that oppressed people, to be truly emancipated, have to liberate themselves.

Gilman spoke most coherently when she called for the rearrangement of middle-class neighborhoods. In the most personal dimension of her social ethics, that concerned with domestic architecture, she was the most profound. When she addressed practical questions of child care and food preparation, her ideas attained a special timelessness. Pleading for herself and her sisters, she discarded pretension in her passion to bring about more democratic environments.

CANCER VICTIM: IMPENDING DEATH AND PREMEDITATED SUICIDE

In January 1932 Gilman learned that she had cancer of the breast. She reported feeling more distress for Houghton than she did for herself since, in her words, "I had not the least objection to dying." Telling her husband of the diagnosis proved to be more difficult than facing it herself. After obtaining medical confirmation that her case was inoperable, Gilman agreed with her distraught husband that she should try X-ray treatment; this therapy reduced her pain and prolonged her life. As she had anticipated, Houghton was very upset about her illness. "He suffered a thousand times more than I did," she wrote.[52] Houghton died very suddenly of a cerebral hemorrhage on May 4, 1934.

In the fall of 1934, Gilman flew to Pasadena to be near her daughter Katharine Stetson Chamberlin and her family for the last year of her life. Grace Channing Stetson came and stayed with Gilman in a very modest little house on South Catalina Avenue during Gilman's last months. The two friends were just two doors down the street from the Chamberlins. Even as she suffered from shingles and the steady encroachment of her cancer, becoming in the end literally speechless, Gilman reveled in the luxuriance of sights and smells in her back yard and maintained her sense of humor.

Gilman ended her own life on Saturday, August 17, 1935, rather than suffer the final ravages of her disease. Shortly after learning the nature and seriousness of her illness, she had begun collecting enough chloroform to use as a substitute means of death when she became sure that the time was right and her usefulness over. She copied a suicide she had admired upon hearing of it for its painlessness and relative neatness: Lying down on her bed, she placed a choloroform mask over her face, the fumes of which quietly killed her.[53] In accordance with Gilman's wishes, her family and friends had no funeral service for her; after the body was cremated, her ashes were scattered in her beloved southern California hills.

CHAPTER THREE

Gilman's Attention to Domestic Architecture: Her Fourfold Case against Prevailing Household Design

Are you content with work,—to toil alone,
To clean things dirty and to soil things clean;
To be a kitchen-maid, be called a queen,—
    Queen of a cook-stove throne?

Are you content to reign in that small space—
A wooden palace and a yard-fenced land—
With other queens abundant on each hand,
    Each fastened in her place?

· · · · · · · · · · · · · · · ·

What holds You? Ah, my dear, it is your throne,
Your paltry queenship in that narrow place,
Your antique labors, your restricted space,
    Your working all alone!

"To the Young Wife"
CHARLOTTE PERKINS STETSON

Charlotte Gilman had an ear for the language of architecture, especially the authoritarian speech of the single-family home. She "heard" the voices behind the walls of disconnected dwellings, voices demanding a self-contained life style based on repetitive, maximum consumption. She recognized the power of the domestic environment either to inflict punishment or to liberate energies, to separate people or to bring them together. She noticed the importance of household design in determining both one's pattern of relationships and one's deployment of time. She had an unusually strong spatial consciousness, reflecting both her artistic and her sociological sensibilities.

Throughout her life, Gilman experienced a stimulating variety of domestic environments. Looking back, she attributed her geographical perspective to mobility. "Never having had a settled home," she wrote, " . . . I have been better able to judge dispassionately and to take a more long-range view of human affairs than is natural to more stationary people."[1] Most of the nineteen buildings she had called "home" by the age of eighteen required Herculean labors to sustain; as a girl, she was initiated into the traditional rigors of daily fire tending, laundry, cleaning, and food preparation. As guest in the homes of Beecher women, her participation in domesticity was sweetened by discussions with respected seniors who took household work very seriously.

The most unusual place Gilman lived as a youth was a Swedenborgian cooperative house in Providence. Her mother, brother, and she moved there when she was almost fifteen and stayed for about a year and a half. Here they lived with two other families and a single man, sharing both household work and social activities. Although in later life she favored commercial forms of domestic organization, her experience in the unconventional household at No. 1 Major Street greatly widened her conception of home.

Although many first-generation women college graduates experienced the conflict Gilman experienced as a young married woman between the "family claim" and the "social claim," her architectural response to the crisis was an unusually creative one. She wanted, intensely, both a lifelong career of public service and the unique satisfactions of friendship and family life. In her perception, the spatial circumstances of her life were preventing such a combination. Early in her first marriage, the design of

Side view of residence at northwest corner of Manning and Ives streets, Providence, Rhode Island, in which Gilman lived in 1875. Penciled arrow on photo indicates the location of her third-floor room. She noted in her photo album that she had written the poem beginning "From my high window the outlooker sees" from this vantage point.

her home had almost driven her mad. She had the imagination to see that the pattern of walls, streets, and even entire neighborhoods could recognize women's desire for public life instead of physically confining them to a narrow sphere.

As a single parent in California, Gilman spent years of her life doing very long hours of solitary domestic work every day, as well as relatively lighter years in domestic collaboration with women friends. Running the boardinghouse in Oakland in 1892 and 1893, filling simultaneous roles as nurse, cook, cleaner, hostess, mother, writer, and public speaker, was particularly strenuous. In contrast, living next door to the Channings, and with Delle Knapp and Helen Campbell, had greatly relieved both the intensity of labor and the isolation of conventional household management. Likewise, the five years (1895–1900) she spent in midlife without regular domestic duties confirmed her sense that the reorganization of housework was crucial to the liberation of women.

Following her second marriage in 1900, Gilman lived in New York City for twenty-two years, at four upper West Side addresses in Manhattan. For six of those years, she and Houghton lived in a building called the Avondale on Seventy-sixth Street at Amsterdam. During this period their apartment was serviced by a commercial kitchen; they ate their meals in a different building down the street at Columbus Avenue. She later recalled that arrangement as exemplary:

> We had "a home without a kitchen," all the privacy and comfort, none of the work and care—except for beds and a little cleaning. We all went out together to breakfast, then Houghton went to his office and Katharine to her school, while I had the morning for my work. I met Katharine for lunch there, and at night we met Houghton at the train and dined together in peace. We had a table to ourselves, but found much entertainment in the talk of the other boarders. When we had a visitor all that was necessary was another $5.00 a week, no trouble at all.[2]

During another three-year period, Gilman retained two servants with whose help she provided room and board to several paying guests.

During her long residency in Manhattan, Gilman was struck by the obvious potential for connected domestic facilities in densely populated areas. She loved the idea of the apartment hotel in which each private unit, of whatever size, was serviced by shared facilities for dining, child care, and maintenance. She actively promoted the development of such living arrangements, explaining how their amenities could be adapted for farming people and residents of small towns and suburbs as well.

Gilman's diverse experience of "home" was the foundation for a lifelong passion for change in the design of residential buildings. Such backbreaking misery as she had known as a young woman was a curse. She would deliver other women from it. Such painful conflict as she had experienced in her first marriage between her work and her family served as a mighty galvanizing force, bracing her commitment to preach and to teach. She recognized the enemy—the material organization of the home—as a complex and subtle one. It was the idol whose tending diverted women from their solemn duties of world service. Although its defenses appeared stout and formidable, Gilman consistently addressed it with humor and courage; the idol must be overthrown.

THE SCOPE OF GILMAN'S CASE AGAINST CONVENTIONAL HOUSING DESIGN

Gilman challenged the prevailing organization of households structurally. Suspicious of "superwoman" solutions, she insisted that her objections to the home as a woman trap could not be met by citing the exceptional person who managed to combine outside work and housekeeping. This was a sociological, not an individual, problem, an urgent public issue, a "world question."[3] She warned against the futility of attempting to improve one's domestic situation in the context of detached residential buildings. "What we must recognize," she argued, "is that, while the conditions remain, the conduct cannot be altered." No one is to blame, she insisted, for the general unrest and dissatisfaction with the home as it is. Others blamed men for their absence, or women for their lack of diligence, or the lazy servant. "We have never thought," she wrote in 1898, "to blame the institution itself, and see whether it could not be improved upon."[4]

In her discussions of household design, Gilman primarily addressed the circumstances of people in the upper and middle classes. In so doing she saw herself as part of a collaborative campaign for socialized neighborhoods. She was counting on the efforts of friends like Helen Campbell and Jane Addams to improve the surroundings of the poorest and most vulnerable classes. Supporting their efforts and they hers, she tried to reach people who had enough money to build the advanced domestic facilities in which they all believed.

The "average home" whose structure Gilman attacked was one in which the wife-mother managed the household and child care while the husband-father earned a living for himself and his family elsewhere. Believing that the life styles of prosperous Americans had a normative function in society as a whole, she aimed to educate people like herself about the errors in their patterns of work and home. She expected them then to build revolutionized communities that could be replicated for all Americans.

Gilman knew that hers was a difficult case to make. She recognized in a deeply existential way the tenacity of "our habit of mother service." For centuries, the association of womanhood and domestic service had been internalized by women, as a duty to be performed, and by men, as daily rights to be expected. As she wrote in about 1930, "We have so mixed motherhood with house-service that we find it difficult to dissociate them."[5] In her most realistic moments, Gilman recognized that men would not relinquish their domestic privileges without a fight, nor would women readily demand them.

Not only had women and men grown accustomed to the habit of female personal service. Gilman realized that the cult of domesticity was actively falsifying the home by representing it as a remote valley hidden from "the pouring stream of social progress."[6] She observed that the aura of holy timelesssness imputed to the home was effectively blunting progressive efforts to reform it. She noted that

> Our thrones have been emptied, and turned into mere chairs for passing presidents. Our churches have been opened to the light of modern life, and the odor of sanctity has been freshened with sweet sunny air. We can see room for change in these old sanctuaries, but none in the sanctuary of the home. And this temple, with its rights [*sic*], is so closely interwound with the services of subject woman, its altar so demands her ceaseless sacrifices, that we find it impossible to conceive of any other basis of human living.[7]

She offered her services, over many decades, as scientific social critic.

Through the years, Gilman gained a reputation as an iconoclast because of the sarcastic barbs she aimed at conventional domestic platitudes. In her poetry and prose, she mocked all sentiment that disguised the brutally hard work women did in their homes. "When we sing," she wrote, "with tears in our eyes and a catch in our voices, 'Home, sweet home, there's no place like home!' we do not mean, 'Housework, sweet housework, there's nothing like housework!' "[8] Her poems often addressed popular domestic traditions maintained at women's expense.

> The wood-box hath no sanctity;
>   No glamour gilds the coal;
> But the Cook-Stove is a sacred thing
> To which a reverent faith we bring
>   And serve with heart and soul.

> The Home's a temple all divine,
>   By the Poker and the Hod!
> The Holy Stove is the altar fine,
> The wife the priestess at the shrine—
>   Now who can be the god?[9]

Despite the difficulty of the case she was making, Gilman's hope was sustained by her convictions about social evolution. Insisting that she was not proposing that society "destroy the home, any more than that we destroy the woman," she maintained that hers would be a modest, unthreatening, evolutionary revision, involving merely that the "*relative position*" of women and home be changed.[10] Just as textiles had once been spun and woven in the "primitive household" and subsequently removed to the "evolved" factory, Gilman believed that all the other domestic industries would gradually be transferred out of the home to centralized commercial facilities.

Gilman challenged her readers and audiences to examine critically each item in the prevailing domestic mythology: the superiority of home cooking, the advantage of child care as performed by a child's own overworked mother, the virtue involved in slaving for one's family, the peace and quiet to be had in the family household, and so on. In fact, she insisted, "we sit starved, cramped, smothered, holding onto what we imagine is the ideal of home life."[11] She believed that she would succeed in convincing people of the validity of her domestic reconstruction proposals only if she could first prove that the contemporary home was wrongly organized.

GILMAN'S FOUR-COUNT INDICTMENT AGAINST THE ORGANIZATION OF THE HOME

Gilman's complaint against the home rested essentially on four critical points. She was hopeful that once she had laid bare the faulty framework of the detached household, people would allow it to collapse of its own dead weight. They could then turn with her to the creation of progressive homes, built on the rock of egalitarian gender relations.

The Home Is Unevolved

Gilman maintained that the industrial plan of a single-family home was "like a clam in a horse-race":[12] it was so anachronistic as to be ridiculous. It called for the simultaneous execution of several "contradictory trades"—cooking, cleaning, caring for children, and so on—all "in one small building" or set of rooms. A generation earlier, Zina Peirce and the Cambridge Cooperative Housekeepers had likewise criticized the conventional home for its lack of specialization. To show the absurdity of so arranging domestic life, Gilman drew an analogy from the world of commerce.

> As separate businesses we can plainly see their incompatibility. No man advertises a "Restaurant and Laundry," or "Bakery and Bathhouse"—the association of fresh food and soiled linen or unclean bodies would not be pleasant to our minds. Neither should we patronize a "Kindergarten and Carpet Cleaning Establishment," or "Primary School and Dressmaking Parlor," and above all, should we avoid a dormitory for adults which was at the same time a nursery for infants. In the care of the sick, for their sakes as well as the other interests involved, we isolate them as far as possible; a hospital naturally striving for quiet and cleanliness.[13]

By looking at them as discrete functions, she proposed to help straighten out "the clumsy tangle of rudimentary industries that are supposed to accompany the home."[14]

One of the evils of the unevolved home, Gilman charged, was its enormous waste. She believed that the facts of home waste, once publicized, would be so appalling to the American business sense as to provoke immediate reform. The most cruel loss to Gilman was that of productive labor, women's labor. That each separate woman in each separate home was laboring long days in lonely isolation, reduplicating herself ad infinitum, was to her a scandalous inefficiency.

Gilman was convinced that home management and child rearing would have been taken with much greater seriousness had they not been regarded as the exclusive responsibility of women. Because of its low valuation of female labor power, society did not object to the glaring loss created by the domestic system. "If they were not women," she wrote, "these innumerable cooks, this fifty per cent of the human race deliberately set aside to cook for the other fifty, no sane economist could bear the thought of such a colossal waste of labor."[15] She praised the higher efficiency of a ship's crew, a lumber camp, and a company of soldiers, each of which hired approximately one cook for fifty people. She compared a hypothetical house-husband, performing each domestic industry himself, to a more enlightened one who specialized, organized, and combined with other men. Does the former love his family more? she asked rhetorically. She pointed out that "If half the men in the world stayed at home to wait on the other half, the loss in productive labor would be that between half and the fraction required to do the work under advanced conditions, say one-twentieth."[16] Based on her calculations, the present organization of the home wasted far too much of the productive labor of the world.

Another form of waste was material. According to her "most modest computation," the conventional domestic system was costing three times what it should be costing. Put another way, two-thirds of what was being spent was being wasted. Where did it go? To pay for "endless repetition of 'plant'" in kitchens, pantries, laundries, and servants' quarters; for rent, fuel, appliances, utensils, dishes, breakage, and food, all of which could be used more efficiently and bought more economically in wholesale, rather than in the smallest retail, quantities. Gilman was convinced that the prevailing domestic system wasted more time, strength, and money than any system imaginable save strict individual isolation.[17]

The unevolved home was also unhealthy, Gilman argued. The food produced by ignorant, unspecialized, amateur cooks could not be expected to meet high standards of nutrition and taste, and it did not. The presence in each home of an active cooking stove produced smoke and grease, which was unhealthy, sometimes dangerous, and always messy. The food-production industries in each home attracted houseflies and assorted other pests and vermin, which were a threat to the health of "the inmates."[18] The absence of efficient housecleaning and laundry services resulted in an excess of dust and lint, which was not conducive to human well-being.

The several operations associated with feeding people were the most serious affront to social progress, in Gilman's estimation. The individualized kitchen, around which family women's industrial lives revolved— planning meals, purchasing food, putting food away, preparing food,

Now, how does the account compare?
By the domestic method:

Rent $1,500
Food 1,664
Labor 960
Fuel and light........................... 50
Interest and depreciation................ 50
                                        ─────
                                        $4,224

This sum is paid for crowded houses full of ill-adjusted industries, for uncertain, low class labor, and constant care and worry.

By organized industry:

Rent $1,200
Food, served........................... 785
Fuel and light.........................   25
Laundry and cleaning................... 265
Child culture.......................... 550
Club dues.............................. 300
                                        ─────
                                        $3,120

To demonstrate the superiority of combined housekeeping facilities, Gilman often offered comparative budgets suggesting that sharing would result in substantial economies to individual families. She included these particular figures in an early twentieth-century article entitled "Domestic Economy."

serving food, cleaning up after meals, storing food—was the primary obstacle to modernization. How appalling that most women had the responsibility for producing "ten hundred and ninety five meals in a year!" She summed up the situation as follows: "The center of difficulty in the home is the kitchen. In it and its perverse and irregular functioning lies the main source of the expense of housekeeping, the labor of housekeeping, the dirt, disease, difficulty, worry, uncertainty, and general unpleasantness incident to housekeeping—in fact, we might better describe the business as 'kitchen keeping.'"[19] Because she pointed to the food-associated processes as the worst problem in residential design, Gilman's comprehensive domestic program was often labeled, as a shortcut, "kitchen-less homes."

The first strand of Gilman's argument thus maintained that the typical American household was defective because it was isolated, unspecialized, wasteful, and unhealthy, in short, because it was unevolved. "Back of history," she wrote, "at the bottom of civilization, untouched by a thousand whirling centuries, the primitive woman, in the primitive home, still toils at her primitive tasks." The conventional organization of the home, in her view, was a major obstacle to the magnificent unfolding of social progress.[20]

The Home Is Unfair to Women

The heart of Gilman's case against prevailing neighborhood design demonstrated its injustice to women. Existing architecture reinforced the nineteenth-century sexual division of labor—to men the world, to women the home—which was patently unfair to women. The segregation of women to housework was doing them incalculable harm. She documented the injurious conditions under which women typically worked in the home. In addition, she demonstrated the effects of these conditions on women's character and range of life choices.

Gilman taught that it was not fair to expect a woman, when she married, to become a nurse, "a private servant, cook, cleaner, mender of rents, a valet, janitor, and chambermaid."[21] This mandatory, lifelong servitude was profoundly inhibiting, humiliating, and harmful to its victims. To communicate her outrage she suggested a comparison. "To visualize it let us reverse the position. Let us suppose that the conditions of home life required every man upon marriage to become his wife's butler—footman—coachman—cook; every man, all men, necessarily following the profession of domestic servants. This is an abhorrent, an incredible idea. So is the other. That an entire sex should be the domestic servants of the other sex is . . . incredible."[22]

In the first place, the work assigned to the domestic worker was undesirable drudgery. There was the daily dealing with dirt. "All that is basest and foulest she in the last instance must handle and remove. Grease, ashes, dust, foul linen, and sooty ironware—among these her days must pass."[23] Besides the basic unpleasantness of the home industries, there was the disesteem women inevitably earned even by performing their assignments well. "However legalized, hallowed, or ossified by time, the position of a domestic servant is inferior."[24]

In the second place, the roles assigned to the homemaker were inharmonious and discordant, requiring the worker to live "a patchwork life." "She lives," Gilman wrote, "in incessant effort to perform all at once and in the same place the most irreconcilable processes. She has to adjust, disadjust, and readjust her mental focus a thousand times a day; not only to things, but to actions; not only to actions, but to persons; and so, to live at all, she must develop a kind of mind that does *not object to discord*."[25] The household manager, under existing conditions, had to relinquish all ambition to concentration or specialization, so constant and diverse were the clamorous demands for her attention, time, and energy.

To maintain the contradictory currents of home life, society used women "as a sort of universal solvent." Gilman tried to show that "this position of holding many diverse elements in solution is not compatible with the orderly crystallization of any of them, or with much peace of mind to the unhappy solvent." The homemaker spent her days in an unpredictable, disorderly, crisscross fashion, repeatedly having to change gears quickly "from cooking to cleaning, from cleaning to sewing, from sewing to nursing, from nursing to teaching, and so, backward, forward, crosswise and over again from morning to night."[26]

This work was exhausting to mind, muscle, and nerve. It was no wonder that the housekeepers of the day were suffering from fatigue, ill health, and early death. Of the average housewife, Gilman wrote, "She works unceasingly; . . . 'No noonings—no evenings—no rainy days!' She works harder and longer than the man, in a miscellaneous shifting field of effort far more exhausting to vitality than his specialised line; *and she bears children too!*"[27] The conventional home epitomized a sweatshop, whose working conditions were not regulable, in which there was no such thing (even in dreams) as an eight-hour day.

Thus Gilman characterized the injury inflicted by society on those who must supervise the "dainty domestic vampire" with its "insatiate demands." The injustice involved was a matter of gender, coercing the "inferior" female into this unevolved and cruel occupational circumstance. Only women had to choose, once and for all, between marriage-domesticity, on the one hand, and independence-career on the other. This injustice had outlasted many others because people generally "still believe in the old established order," which prescribed "woman's ordination to the service of bodily needs of all sorts," she wrote in 1903.[28]

To prove the unfairness of these expectations, Gilman went on to speak about the ways in which female personality development was impeded by the conditions of home life. She argued that the automatic social assignment of women to domesticity, regardless of individual talent, was an "unnatural separation of falsely divided classes," resulting in the creation of "rudimentary women and more highly developed men." She believed that the injustice could best be recognized by looking without sentimentality at "the distorted nature of the creature[s]" themselves, most of whom were "weak and little women, with the aspirations of an affectionate guinea pig." She proceeded to document the handicaps of women who composed "a starved and thwarted class."[29]

Women's first developmental handicap was that they were economically dependent upon men, owing to the necessities of the present organization of the home. The occupational structures of society presupposed that most women would get their living by getting a husband. The "sexuo-economic" dependency of women caused them to overdevelop themselves as sexual beings and to neglect themselves as autonomous, rational individuals, which was to do themselves harm.

Wanting both to avoid the domestic frustrations of her mother and to emulate the scholarly achievements of her father, Gilman firmly believed that productive labor was the sine qua non of human life. Reflecting the mainstream of the nineteenth-century women's movement, she taught that working at the task for which one has a special aptitude was a basic human right. Self-respect, in her view, depended upon being self-supporting. Therefore, she was indignant that women, the forced housekeepers and child rearers of the world, had "not been allowed to specialize and develop genius."[30] They had been "clipped like a hedge to a low uniformity."[31] They had had to endure "the aching, quenchless misery of work denied."[32] Limited to personal service in a narrow sphere, women had been robbed of their individual identity as productive citizens. They had been rewarded instead for playing the unnatural role of "priestess of the temple of consumption."[33] Evolved, progressive homes, she insisted, would cater to the needs of women who go to work outside them.

According to Gilman, a second developmental handicap suffered by women/house-servants was having brains atrophied by nonuse and confinement to the home. She was concerned throughout her life to prove that women were the intellectual equals of men, despite the fact that the material conditions of the home had retarded their mental proficiency to date. In 1903 she wrote, "We have called the broader, sounder, better balanced, more fully exercised brain 'a man's brain,' and the narrower, more emotional and personal one 'a woman's brain'; whereas the difference is merely that between the world and the house."[34] Nine years later, in *Our Brains and What Ails Them,* she continued the argument with an analogy to Chinese foot binding. "The daughter may inherit the brain of a line of scholars, as a Chinese woman may inherit the legs of a line of runners; but the 'female leg' in China has been sadly modified *by its environment*—and so has 'the female mind.' "[35]

Gilman detailed the effects of home conditions on female intelligence. She traced connections between the woman's role as the personal servant of others and "her greater sensitiveness to all personal events." She pointed out that it was not surprising that a person whose daily round consisted of "a varying zigzag horde of little things" should lack perseverance and singleness of mind.[36]

Gilman argued against those who maintained that "the feminine mind" was innately "more submissive, less critical, less argumentative, less experimental," lacking in "initiative." She insisted that purveyors of this erroneous view were describing "not a sex-mind, but a class mind" and, to drive the point home, suggested that

> If man had been arbitrarily divided into two classes; if half of them had been given the range of all the trades, crafts, arts and sciences, all education, all experience, and achievement, and the other half shut up at home, never allowed out alone, and taken under escort to only a small part of life's attractions; confined exclusively to a few primitive industries; denied education as well as experience, we would find mysterious, subtle, baffling differences between the two classes.[37]

In a poem entitled "The Housewife," Gilman probed connections she saw between a woman's houseservice on the one hand and her intellectual limitations on the other.

Food and the serving of food—that is my daylong care;
What and when we shall eat, what and how we shall wear;
Soiling and cleaning of things—that is my task in the main—
Soil them and clean them and soil them—soil them and clean them
again.

To work at my trade by the dozen and never a trade to know;
To plan like a Chinese puzzle—fitting and changing so;
To think of a thousand details, each in a thousand ways;
For my own immediate people and a possible love and praise.

My mind is trodden in circles, tiresome, narrow and hard,
Useful, commonplace, private—simply a small back-yard;
And I the Mother of Nations!—Blind their struggle and vain!—
I cover the earth with my children—each with a housewife's
brain.[38]

Although Gilman believed that society had seriously injured women in
these various ways, she also believed that women shared part of the
responsibility for the wrong. In *Pernicious Adam,* for example, she spoke
about "our major sin of omission: our failure to use our minds."[39] Women
had not applied their wits to the rational solution of these problems, and,
in Gilman's view, it was time for them all to begin thinking critically and
taking responsibility for them.

The third personality handicap of the woman/house-servant, thus
alluded to, was her moral dwarfhood. She did not know how to be an
independent self. Women, in Gilman's view, had become "poor, care-
hardened, home-dwarfed creatures—whose eyes, long used to a small
dark space, can see nothing outside but a glare." Under such conditions it
was no wonder that women should see themselves as "here to make
people—not to be people!"[40] Because she had been confined to the
domestic sphere, woman had not developed the capacity to think and act
collectively. She had not learned to address herself to public problems. She
had not aspired to fully human virtues or embraced, as her own responsibility, the duties of world citizenship. She had not begun to learn the
urgent subtleties of social ethics, so absorbed was she in the ABCs of home
management. Gilman saw this handicap as a brutal oppression: "this
savage limitation to the personal, and mainly to the physical," which "we
have so rigidly enforced upon women," this "keeping woman a social
idiot."[41]

Gilman thus set forth the injustice of locking women into the ignominious toils of primitive housework. Firmly believing in the essential greatness of women—their capacity for genius in all areas, their human dignity and intelligence—she traced the actual moral, industrial, and intellectual puniness of women to the material conditions in their homes. She hoped that the logic of her case would appeal to men, whose good will she assumed, and to women, whose residual courage and ambition she took for granted.

The Home Injures All Its Inmates

Gilman believed that the prevailing organization of the home did serious damage to all its inhabitants and not just to women. She called attention to the injustice of the husband-father's heavy economic responsibilites. She cited the home's inauspicious circumstances for relaxation, its daily hardships for marriage. She found fault with domestic methods of child care. She believed that the unsatisfactory physical and social conditions in the home adversely affected everyone within it.

Convinced that every adult human being was intended by nature to be economically self-sufficient, Gilman was appalled that the cost of maintaining a detached dwelling required adult males to shoulder their wives' as well as their own fiscal burdens. What was a "prison,—a workhouse—and a consuming fire" to women was a "millstone" to men. Because they were so expensive, she reasoned, strictly private housekeeping patterns were requiring men to choose their work strictly on the basis of its remuneration instead of its social service. She lamented the resulting social treason.[42]

To Gilman, the idea (later to become a trade union demand) of a "family wage," sufficient to support an entire family, as the payment due a male worker, was an abomination. She agreed that prevailing economic demands, generated by the wasteful organization of domesticity, were "mercilessly" overwhelming for a man. But the solution to the problem should certainly not be to pay men enough to perpetuate a wasteful, unjust system. The correct solution, according to Gilman, would start with democratic neighborhood designs with conveniently located, shared domestic services. In addition, she sounded a battle cry for all women to step forward to assume their fair share (half) of the economic responsibility for their families' needs.

The "private" home perpetrated other forms of injury to men. They could expect to be ill fed. Malnutrition resulted from the fact that perpetual amateurs did the planning, buying, and preparing of food. There was no nutritionist in most homes. Besides eating poorly, men could expect to eat too much. Overeating resulted from having one's own personal cook; not surprisingly, these cooks often became overinvested in their cuisine.

Furthermore, under present conditions, men were encouraged to become "ultra-males," selfish and proud to a degree unthinkable in women. Gilman argued that, whereas "mother-service" when directed to young offspring was natural and good, "mother-service" when directed at grown males was unnatural and wicked. The excessive self-centeredness of males was fostered and perpetuated by the "body service" rendered by homebound women. Possessing a fellow human, whose purpose in life was to please and serve, was a powerful stimulant to the exaggeration of one's ego.[43]

Gilman believed that the industrial organization of the home undermined, if not destroyed, companionship and pleasure between husband and wife. Present domestic conditions, in her view, even fostered intense incompatibility between them; because of the exaggerated dichotomy between home and world, their relationship was subject to nettlesome irritation at all times.

Gilman taught that marriage could be a perfect union only when occurring between "class equals." She documented two types of incompatibility in conventional marriages, socioeconomic and moral-spiritual. Describing the first disparity, she argued that a married couple could expect to be socially unequal since men as a rule were working in highly specialized, evolved occupations whereas women were confined to strictly unspecialized, unevolved industrial positions. "They are economically on entirely different social planes," said Gilman.[44] Characterizing the underlying moral-spiritual discordancy in conventional marriage, she maintained that it resulted from a breakdown in communication between man's larger "world consciousness" and woman's narrow "domestic consciousness." They were dissonant with each other. Looking at both sides, she suggested that "The woman is narrowed by the home and the man is narrowed by the woman."[45]

Gilman argued that the "constant friction" and waste of nervous energy in marriage were due to the industrial conditions in which they were located. "The running of the commissary and dormitory departments of life, with elaborate lavatory processes," was exacting, exhausting work, all the more taxing for persons untrained in its several techniques. Management details concerning the successful financing and execution of the day-to-day household routine often absorbed all the time and energy a married couple had together, leaving none for mutual enrichment and common pursuits. "A house does not need a wife," she insisted, "any more than it does a husband. Are we never to have a man-wife? A really suitable and profitable companion for a man instead of the bond-slave of a house?"[46]

Gilman believed that the home environment was doing harm to children, too. Convinced that the first few years of a child's life were of utmost formative importance, she judged that there was no human endeavor more worthy of excellence and esteem than "the right education of children." She attacked prevailing child-care arrangements primarily for two circumstances.

In the first place, children were not receiving quality nurture and edification. Mothers and fathers were so preoccupied with details relating to the care of creature comforts that they did not have time to relate to their children as persons, much less to understand and enjoy them. The inefficient organization of the home was such that the work of cooking, cleaning, and maintenance held center stage, requiring children to remain in the wings, making do with leftover scraps of time and energy. Gilman believed that since the household industries were incompatible with quality "child culture," the two should be disengaged from each other and relocated in more suitable environments.

Gilman taught that "child specialists" with a high degree of talent, training, and actual experience with children should be involved in children's lives from early infancy. Since persons possessing these qualities were rare, she suggested that those few who were so gifted should be encouraged to socialize their skills, employing them in the service of children from many families. If they were to focus such ability on one child or only a few, she believed, the resulting atmosphere would be too intense for healthy growth; the effect would be like that produced by "an ever-enlarging burning glass, still focussed upon one spot."[47]

In the second place, the home was preventing children from learning the meaning of social justice. Since the confinement of women as house-servants was unfair, children were learning not to question injustice, indeed to depend upon it. Gilman observed that the harassed mother (or the more affluent "parasitical" mother), although well-meaning, tended to indulge her children, relating to them in ways "too conciliatory and self-denying"; that the organization of the home communicated to the child that he was the center of the universe, for whom this overworked woman was pouring out her life and love. Gilman believed that the maternal passion, "like all passions . . . needs conscientious and rational restraint."[48] She was convinced that the sacrificial devotion of a mother too often weakened the child's sense of justice while teaching him to be selfish.

The third strand of Gilman's argument thus contended that everyone who lived in a typical, unconnected household, whether man, woman, or child, was sustaining physical and spiritual injury due to its obsolete organization. In addition to the several issues enumerated above, Gilman criticized the home for its "parlor-mindedness," its failure to promote truly uplifting, honest, social discourse. Residents of conventional homes were too often satisfied with the banal and superficial practices of "entertaining" and "receiving," practices commonly and ironically known as "society." For Gilman, "the soft wavelets and glassy shallows of polite conversation" were no substitute for the worldly-wise social interchange appropriate to responsible, modern people.

The Home Precludes Social Morality

Gilman was convinced that conventional housing design prevented the development of social ethics. No part of her argument was more important to her. She believed that all resistance to social progress had its ultimate source in the "primitive" home. She maintained that all indifference to the improvement of society could be traced to that hotbed of personalism, the detached, self-contained family household. Until people recognized the necessity of profound organizational changes at home, she insisted it was futile to hope for the eradication of social ills in the world outside it.

According to Gilman, the root of the problem lay in the ultraspecialization of women to domestic roles inside the home. Because they lived most of their lives within its four walls, women had little opportunity (and no encouragement) to develop a morality that encompassed more than the home and its inhabitants. Women's lifelong preoccupation with personal service led to a narrow, distorted view of the world. Women were unable to recognize an evil condition for what it was. Instead of the condition itself, they would look for a bad individual on whom to pin the blame for a particular evil. Because of their intimate relationship to husbands and children, it was inevitable that women should inculcate personalistic values, teaching a strictly private ethic day by day, subtly and irresistibly.

The home's "primitive" organization, in Gilman's reading of it, trained its inhabitants to be vigilantly attentive to interpersonal duties and heedlessly ignorant of collective ones. It was not inappropriate for family members to relate to each other in a personal mode, learning in so doing the skills and duties of kinship and affection. It *was* inappropriate, however, to consider one's larger social obligations simply in terms of categories and skills learned in the family.

The overlearning of personalist morality caused two kinds of misunderstanding about which Gilman was concerned. In the first place, people were incapable of recognizing sins perpetrated against society. Alert to the intricacies of stepping on another individual's toes, people were oblivious to the fact that they could (and did) injure the social organism itself. Whereas a "moral" person would scrupulously avoid picking flowers or dumping garbage in a neighbor's yard, he would not hesitate (or suffer a twinge of conscience) from ravaging the uninhabited countryside by taking and dumping.

The ultrapersonal ethical consciousness engendered by domestic circumstances had no means of restraining people from polluting waterways and otherwise damaging the common weal. To illustrate this point, Gilman wrote: "The housewife sees the dust on her parlor table, but she does not see the smoke and cinders that blacken her city. She sees that little Willy is looking tired. She does not see that all the school children are overworked. She sees that her daughter's health has broken down after marriage. She does not see that all girls should know the chances and dangers of marriage before it is too late."[49] Society itself, and particular groups within it, were being sinned against in serious ways, and Gilman sounded an alarm.

The second shortcoming of ultrapersonal morality was its failure to account for collectivities as valid agents of responsibility. Gilman tried to show her fellow Americans that they could not think collectively, as a whole people, because one-half of them (women) were systematically confined to the private realm. Searching inappropriately for culpable individuals, people failed to grasp the fact of corporate guilt. Part of the problem was that the public was accustomed to thinking of a sin as a unified whole, with a beginning, an end, and a single perpetrator. In modern, industrialized society, Gilman realized, crimes had become more fractional and complex. Many people were implicated in one way or another, for example, "in the deaths of a few screaming tenants of firetrap tenements."[50] Likewise, every person of means was responsible for what happened to the least privileged. "Children born in slums," she wrote, "reared in ignorance, poverty, and dirt become criminals not because they are wicked, but because we are, we, the social group which maintains criminal-breeding conditions."[51]

Gilman believed that, in a democracy, responsibility for society's welfare rested on all the people. As long as mothers and fathers cared only for their own offspring, she reasoned, society could expect to have criminals and "ne'er-do-wells" of various sorts. Mothers, she argued, must learn the lessons of "social parentage." Fathers, in her view, more nearly exemplified social parentage because of their advanced industrial status as specialized workers. Men had come to realize that they could serve their own and all children best by working at their appropriate life station outside the home. Gilman called for mothers to follow suit by relinquishing control over their own children's lives, pursuing instead their particular, individulized work on behalf of all the world's children.

Gilman conveyed a sense of the family as a collective, moral entity. According to her conception of social responsibility, the family was found guilty—of gross self-indulgence and self-preoccupation, of frantic consumerism, of immoral insularity and aloofness from the world around it. Isolated homes prevented people from seeing society as a whole and recognizing its needs for redistribution and reform. Homes were the objects of idolatry, the center of the rationale justifying the immolation of women. The people living in conventional homes were accountable for the moral consequences of their living arrangements.

To promote progressive social change. Gilman recommended a universalistic sense of responsiblity in place of domestic-mindedness. She urged people to embrace the whole world as their dwelling.[52] She believed that the capacity to see correctly and act responsibly could not be achieved under present domestic conditions. " 'An only child is apt to be selfish.' So is an only family," she insisted.[53] Not until neighborhoods were built according to unified blueprints could social awareness and justice be achieved, she maintained. Domestic morality, in terms of which people hopelessly tried to comprehend the modern situation, urgently needed correction and addition. As she saw it, the revision of residential architecture was a necessary prelude to the development of an adequate social morality.

Along such lines as these, throughout her life, Gilman argued that the home was wrongly organized. She catalogued its inefficiencies, its material and spiritual waste, its resultant obstacles to the achievement of social harmony in general. She elaborated its injustices, this "strangling cradle of the race," most cruelly inhibiting to women, damaging men and children and all institutions under its influence. She described its stifling isolation from social interchange, noting its role in impeding concern for the public good. She urged each household to discontinue its functions as an anti-quated workshop/museum on the one hand and teacher of obsolete morality on the other. She had another model to recommend.

EVALUATING THE POWER OF GILMAN'S INDICTMENT

Gilman's spirited critique of domestic architecture was fueled by her optimistic reading of the social landscape. Like most of her progressive mentors and colleagues, she expected only better, fairer days ahead. In particular, she believed that the invention of hotel-sized refrigerators, stoves, and washing machines had very auspicious implications for the kinds of environments she wanted to see built. Exactly such machinery was perfectly suited for use in the connected household facilities she was promoting.

Gilman's hopefulness was stirred as well by her conviction that the root of industrial society's numerous ills lay in, of all places, the private home. Although it might appear to some that women were not in a very strong position to "improve the world" as she so passionately wanted them to do, Gilman found it credible since domestic reform would, of necessity, originate within their sphere (or stronghold). Although in retrospect her expectations seem naive, it was in fact very bold of her to suggest that the very first step toward economic democracy was to rearrange the spaces over which women had the most control.

Because of their stake in the marginality of women, the institutions of monopoly capitalism were going to offer far more resistance to Gilman's proposals that she could imagine. For a variety of reasons, the American business sense quickly showed itself to be worse than indifferent to the waste of women's labor power so offensive to Charlotte Gilman. And the material waste she documented has gradually come to be recognized as precisely the optimal condition for an unregulated capitalist economy. The conventional domestic model, according to which subordinate women serve the needs of dominant males, has proven, over the decades, to be an invaluable legitimating factor for the sexist distribution of economic opportunity in society at large. The more natural all-women-doing-housework can be made to seem, the less resistance can be expected to the segregation of women in low-paid, servile jobs.

In Gilman's day, as middle-class women fought for the right to work outside the home, few could appreciate that the very occupational structures of society themselves relied very heavily on the "sexuo-economic dependency" of women. She did not understand the importance to corporate profit margins of relegating women to the home, thereby maximizing both their specialization as consumers and their availability as a convenient source of unskilled (compliant) labor when the need arose. Although Gilman recognized important connections between patterns of male dominance inside the home and outside it, she did not comprehend the relationship between women's unpaid domestic work and the daily maintenance of a cheap labor supply for industry. Neither could she see that the jobs of corporate managers, jobs she was strongly encouraging women to seek, presupposed the existence of a doting wife behind the scenes, servicing her mate, caring for their children, having no work in mind herself apart from those very exacting support services.

In the early days of monopoly capitalism, it was harder to grasp the extent to which the entire economic system depends upon an ever-expanding grand total of private consumption. Like Bellamy, she wanted to believe, and did believe, that the state existed to serve and protect people and to look out for the needs of less privileged groups. It has taken more than two generations for feminists to assimilate the fact that the United States government is more committed to protecting the property relations of its far-flung global empire than it is to protecting people and vulnerable groups. Given that relationship, it is no surprise that the state is heavily invested in sustaining the reliable market demands of inefficient, detached households. In light of the expanding consumption potential of conventional neighborhoods, it follows that powerful moneyed interests, and the government that serves them, have been staunch supporters of the architectural status quo.

There were other mistakes in Gilman's analysis, which are much easier to see in retrospect. She greatly romanticized the world of paid work, men's larger, forbidden sphere, which in our day we can see is too often routinized, alienated, and de-skilled, or devastated by unemployment, or dominated by excessively long hours.

Going along with her romanticism about paid work, she was too scornful toward the "unspecialized" home. Although traditional housework *is* taxing, many working-class women would like very much to have the liberty to stay at home. And women who do their own full-time domestic work undoubtedly have very positive work satisfactions, along with the frustrations and difficulties Gilman described so well. As Gilman pointed out, housewives do worry about *"little"* things like "What's for dinner?" and stain removal, but she was wrong to put that down so emphatically. After a "second wave" of feminism, "little" things like meals and laundry are becoming more widely recognized as highly political matters.

Oppressed by the constraints of obligatory domesticity, Gilman did not understand the historic function the private home has played as a center of courageous resistance to forces of repression and greed. Her waspishness, furthermore, seriously diminished her sense of home. Not only did it prevent her from making alliances with people in the New York neighborhoods where she lived; she was also oblivious to the informal cooperative networks, created by blacks and members of other ethnic groups right around her, for domestic and economic survival.

Gilman did not examine the issue of who does housework to any critical extent except to insist that professionals do it. She sometimes seemed to assume that the housework professionals would be women. At other times, she simply did not address the question. What she could not foresee was the way systems of male and class dominance have elaborated millions of jobs for "housework professionals." But instead of rewarding them adequately, financially and socially, the society keeps its janitors, maids, and fast-food workers on the lowest rungs of its occupational ladders.

Despite the limitations of her perspective, Gilman had extraordinary skills as an "environmental skanner."[54] She was a pioneer in suggesting that the built form of society should serve rather than frustrate the needs of employed women. Having seen urban centers at an early, dynamic moment in their development, she was aware of the arbitrariness in the way cities and blocks were laid out. They did not *have* to be built in a given way. Just because they were there did not mean that their form had been inevitable. Such awareness can breed revolution.

CHAPTER FOUR

Gilman's Utopian Portrait of Nonsexist Landscapes

O heavenly world, where folk may breathe
Sweet air from windy hill
Sweet air from ocean swinging free,
Sweet air from desert still—
Why do we live where every breath
Brings thick distaste and coming death!

. . . .

O heavenly world, with room for all,
Wide spaces, Friendship sweet,
Clean solitude, the soul's repose,
True pleasure when we choose to meet—
Why do we live where heaped mankind
Breeds loathing in the crowded mind!

"O Heavenly World!"
CHARLOTTE PERKINS GILMAN

Gilman's lively imagination added a positive dimension to her case for alternative architecture. In the course of her life, she wrote over 100 short stories, novels, and plays. Writing them was frequently associated with economic necessity in her early career; in 1893, for example, she noted in her diary her resolve to "write $5-worth a day." To do so, she followed a work plan in which she set out to spend "say one day of my five a week for a short story—one for a short article—three for more extended work. . . . Poems—as it happens."[1] Intuitively, Gilman recognized the power of fiction to introduce people to unexpected possibilities.

Although most of her stories were written in a vernacular style featuring familiar characters in situations from everyday life, Gilman also wrote half a dozen mythological tales in a more stylized vein. The present chapter discusses three of these more fanciful tales, designating them "utopian." Chapter 7 in turn will examine the more colloquial, easygoing narratives, distinguishing them by the name "realistic."

In the utopian stories, Gilman conjured up a vision of what a prosperous, nonsexist world would look like. With scant attention to details concerning, for example, how it would get built, she here encouraged people to dream with her about the contours of a righteous paradise. She thereby invited people to visualize a built environment that would liberate their human energies instead of exaggerating their gender differences.

Following a look at some of the source of her inspiration, this chapter will explore Gilman's mythic landscapes. After looking at three fictional versions of utopia, it will discuss their most striking features, both common themes and intriguing differences.

GILMAN'S INTRODUCTION TO THE ARCHITECTURAL IMAGINATION

Gilman's consideration of the built environment was encouraged by many of the adults she knew in her youth. Her great-aunt, Catharine Beecher (1800–78), whom Hayden has described as "the most influential woman designer of the century," published blueprints for dozens of household types in her moral-educational campaigns of the 1840s, fifties, and sixties.[2] Although Gilman, in her career, would concentrate on undoing the domestic ideology so sacred to Aunt Catharine, Beecher and her sister,

Harriet Stowe (1811–96), had helped significantly to forge a nineteenth-century ethical idiom in which the remaining household industries were critically analyzed both spatially and morally. Although Gilman's work was much more radical, it can be seen as part of a tradition continuous with that of her great-aunts, one that carefully examined the socioeconomic organization of domesticity.

Gilman was impressed by the public work of her illustrious aunts, taking inspiration in particular from the moral fervor evoked by Stowe's blockbuster novel, *Uncle Tom's Cabin*.[3] Another close family member, Gilman's uncle, Edward Everett Hale (1822–1909), a Unitarian clergyman from Boston, and frequent author, had written a book called *Workingmen's Homes* as well as a utopian novel called *Sybaris* (1869). Hale coached Gilman in public speaking, helping her to launch her career in the Nationalist movement of which he, too, was a member.[4]

During Gilman's youth, the future of the home was a lively topic of concern outside her family as well. Between 1850 and 1875, followers of Fourier and Owen were provoking discussion throughout the United States about their collectivized architectural innovations; illustrations and floor plans depicting their communal housekeeping facilities were published widely in popular magazines during that period.[5]

In the last two decades of the nineteenth century, a book by a socialist in Germany, August Bebel (1840–1913), caused quite a stir among socialist intellectuals in the United States. In *Woman under Socialism* (1883), Bebel called for the state development of massive apartment houses for workers, to be serviced by large eating facilities and child-care centers. Strikingly, Bebel believed that the home should foster the implementation of perfect gender equality. He had no use for insidious distinctions relegating women and men to separate private and public spheres. Optimistic about the potential of factories to obliterate status differences between men and women, he liked to portray the proletarian home of the future as a streamlined adjunct to the factory. Convinced that women had just as much responsibility as men to work for wages, he advocated the complete removal of domestic industries from a family's living quarters.

Bebel was convinced that the household drudgery that preoccupied women would wither away once his reforms were enacted. He argued that a socialist state should create and maintain a complete system of domestic support services connected to kitchenless apartment homes. The proposed system would include factory kitchens and bakeries, mechanical laundries, and state-owned heating, electrical, and plumbing facilities, the pipes of which would be installed in every home. In addition, according to his scheme, "central cleaning establishments" would "see to the dusting," and child-care centers would nurture the young from their earliest years. Seeking to routinize a set of industries that was overly romanticized, he stressed the greater efficiency and hygiene that would accrue from the attachment of workers' homes to the latest cleaning, delivery, and labor-saving machinery. Bebel expected the private kitchen as center of domestic life to be rendered "wholly superfluous" by the centralized institutions for which he stood.[6] In 1896 Gilman appeared on the same speakers' platform with Bebel at a socialist peace demonstration in Hyde Park.[7]

Gilman knew a lot about contemporary experimentation with the built environment. Besides being a voracious reader, she gravitated throughout her life to people concerned with such matters. She also visited many places in which people were practicing alternative life styles.

Neighborhood settlement houses and summer campgrounds greatly stimulated Gilman's imagination. During her visits to Hull House, she observed the vital communal function of shared facilities in working-class residential areas. At Jane Addams's invitation, she spent a brief period in 1895–96 helping Helen Campbell supervise Unity Settlement House (which later became Eli Bates House) on the North Side of Chicago.

Gilman particularly appreciated the social spaces in educational summer resorts like the one in Chatauqua, New York. While visiting several such campgrounds, she delighted in the corporate provision of cooked food in central dining areas. She applauded the organization of daily room cleaning and laundry services for all guests. She admired the lively programs of group activity for everyone from babies to senior citizens. She wanted to replicate such services in every neighborhood on a year-round basis. She argued that everyone's home—and not just occasional vacation spots—should become a sanctuary of refreshing, nurturant leisure.

Besides having read Marie Howland's popularizations of Fourierist architectural innovations, Gilman visited several communitarian socialist settlements. In January and February 1899, she made stops both at N. O. Nelson's "model village of Leclaire," Missouri, and at J. A. Wayland's colony at Ruskin, Tennessee, about fifty miles west of Nashville. Although she found "lots of nice people" at Leclaire, she was emphatically unimpressed with the second community, declaring, "Ruskin was another of those sublimely planned, devotedly joined, and invariably deserted Socialist colonies. Only ignorance of the real nature of social relation can account for these high-minded idiocies."[8] Even though it was clear that the Ruskin Association was in a state of serious decline by the time she visited it, Gilman disdained its efforts. As the century turned, she was more taken with the potential for socialist architecture in dense urban centers than she was with idealistic groups trying to build more rural utopias. And she believed that shrewd business skills would prove to be at least as important as lofty principles in making such alternative communities work.

The urbanism of Bellamy suited Gilman very well. Futuristic Boston was clean, unpolluted, supportive of women's work outside the home, and efficient. Furthermore, Bellamy's poetic treatment of class was meaningful to Gilman. Instead of a hard-headed treatment of economic status, Bellamy depicted society vaguely as a hodgepodge of rich and poor, educated and ignorant. He likened capitalist society to "a prodigious coach" harnessed to the "masses of humanity," carrying the wealthy in idle splendor, driven, cruelly, by "hunger." In the utopia of Bellamy's imagination, all work has miraculously become dignified, the word "menial" has disappeared, and the evenhanded distribution of wealth and economic opportunity has evolved painlessly, resulting in a beatific, egalitarian classlessness.

Gilman was an important recruit to the Nationalist cause. She wholeheartedly supported Bellamy's call for state-supported domestic services as part of a sweeping social transformation. Much like Bellamy, she concerned herself with middle-class life styles. Leaders of the Bellamy movement respected Gilman's personal experience of conventional housekeeping, taking to heart her vivid testimony to its crippling toll. They recognized that her elaborations on the Nationalist case for centralized housekeeping would greatly enhance its authority and appeal.

Over the years, Gilman created her particular vision of socialized homes in conversation with a variety of socialists and feminists. She saw these colleagues as a progressive constituency arising to demand connected environments for work and family life. Serene in the conviction that the irresistible force of social evolution was squarely behind her, she judged the educational programs of middle-class socialist and women's clubs to be the most appropriate channels through which to seek support for her domestic revisions.

Gilman dreamed of an environment in which nature and culture coexisted in beautiful harmony. The built form of her utopian world facilitated an easy equality between men and women. It allowed men to

Drawing by Katharine Stetson showing egalitarian partnership between woman and man both in child raising and in responsibility for the world. Gilman used it as cover for *The Forerunner* during its first year of publication.

enjoy their children's daily company as much as their work. It permitted women to invest themselves more in paid work and projects of social amelioration than in the delivery of incessant household services to their families.

UTOPIA IN FOUR STORIES: FUTURISTIC NEW YORK CITY, CALIFORNIA, AND HERLAND

Three novels and one short story set forth the kind of utopian world Gilman was encouraging people to build. *Moving the Mountain* (1911), *Herland* (1915), and *With Her in Ourland* (1916) all appeared first in serialized form in the *Forerunner*. To accommodate her monthly publishing schedule, the author divided each of these novels into twelve chapters.[9] This deliberate creation of a dozen chapters had the most arbitrary, tedious results in the second Herland story. "Bee Wise" is a short story which Gilman published in the fourth year of the *Forerunner*.

In order to consider Gilman's utopian vision as a whole, it is necessary first to examine the several stories in which she set it forth. Since *Moving the Mountain* was the earliest of this group, as well as the most emphatically urban, it serves as an appropriate starting point. "Bee Wise" comes next chronologically; it is a gem of design detail. The two Herland tales are the most ethereal, the least related to particular places in the United States, the most dreamlike, the least specific about the built environment. Because they were also the last two in this group, their vagueness suggests that Gilman was becoming less confident in her euphoric expectations of evolving American society as the United States prepared to enter the Great War.

Moving the Mountain

When the story opens in the year 1940, John Robertson, the fifty-five-year-old protagonist of *Moving the Mountain,* has just awakened from a thirty-year bout of amnesia. His younger sister, Nellie Robertson, has traveled more than halfway around the world to "Thibet" to locate him. In addition to being a loyal family member, she is both a physician and a college president back in the United States. On a leisurely sea voyage from Asia back to New York City, Nellie informs her awakening brother that a nonviolent, socialist-feminist revolution has dramatically transformed American society during his absence.

Gilman was one of several nineteenth-century utopian novelists who created a protagonist who sleeps through a major social upheaval. Although his tale of the rehabilitation of Boston was the most famous of them, Edward Bellamy had had many precursors in the use of that motif. In her 1836 novel, *Three Hundred Years Hence,* for example, the hero of Mary Griffith's story is buried alive by a volcano and awakens 300 years later in a new, nonsexist Philadelphia.[10] Although his story is not precisely utopian, Washington Irving's hero, Rip van Winkle, has a famous twenty-year sleep, only to awaken after the thirteen British colonies have become the United States of America. In the most astonishing nap of all, John Macnie's hero, in *The Diothas: or, A Far Look Ahead* (1883), takes a snooze for eighty-seven centuries and awakens in a utopian New York City.[11] A businessman/novelist from Lewiston, Maine, Bradford Peck, who was a contemporary of Gilman's, wrote still another book of this type; in *The World a Department Store* (1900), the hero, Percy Brantford, falls asleep (with the aid of sleeping powders) and awakens twenty-five years later after the United States has abandoned capitalism in favor of a cooperative system.

Moving the Mountain recounts the process by which John Robertson becomes acquainted with the "New World" that he finds back in the United States. His brother-in-law, Owen Montrose (profession unspecified), his niece, Hallie Robertson (food inspector), and nephew, Jerrold Montrose (musician), join Dr. Nellie Robertson in extending hospitality to their curious, returning kinsman. They all find amusement in John's sense of dazed incredulity. They go to great lengths to convince him that the dreamlike world he's seeing all around him is very real and much better than the old one (for which he tends to feel nostalgic).

Adding spice to an ongoing stream of didactic conversation, Owen and Nellie take John on extensive sightseeing excursions, explaining everything to him proudly and patiently. To enhance his adjustment to life under nonsexist socialism, they arrange a meeting for him with several scientific "experts," all of whom reinforce the family's upbeat indoctrination. So that his lingering doubts can be dispelled, they take him to see his old friend Frank Borderson. In college, Borderson had been such a wayward, "God-forsaken rascal" that he had been expelled "for improper conduct." Not only has the revised social order recalled this rogue from a life of ruin; it has inspired and trained him to become a "Professor of Ethics" in a university where he has now been teaching for twenty years.

Gilman liked to introduce little flourishes, like this account of Borderson's rehabilitation, to suggest that her dreams were morally superior as well as desirable and achievable.

Like Bellamy's urban utopia, Gilman's consists of a dramatically reformed cityscape. Her Manhattan—like his Boston—is a veritable garden, from the East River to the Hudson, from the Battery to the Bronx. The city's industries and utilities are run entirely on water-powered electricity; there are no dirty smokestacks. The waterways are sparkling and clear blue, providing efficient arteries of transportation for the city's nonpolluting boats and ships. The city's delivery system is soundless, streamlined, clean, and underground, "a silent monorail." All New Yorkers are healthy, sensibly dressed, cultured, engaged in a modest amount of appropriate work, and therefore happy. The average working day is four hours long, even though no one is required to work more than two hours a day. Fathers and mothers alike gambol in the parks with their children in the afternoons. No one is tired or driven, nor is anyone overworked or mistreated.

Nellie Robertson catalogs the miracles of the renovated society to her bewildered brother. Among many other things, she boasts that "there is no such thing in the civilized world as poverty—no labor problem—no color problem—no sex problem—almost no disease—very little accident [*sic*]—practically no fires— . . . no crime."[12] She explains that all of these improvements were made possible by the elimination of fighting and war in the world with the subsequent cancellation of the U.S. military budget. Whereas in the old dispensation, 70 percent of the national revenue had been allocated to defense, in the reformed society all of that money is now spent on progressive domestic programs. Hitherto undreamed of prosperity and plenty, equitably shared, are the delightful result.

A revolutionary "New Food" system is at the center of the new society's neighborhood design. "Food furnishing" companies, featuring nutritious, cooked food, have been established all over the country. Now meals can be purchased either at a neighborhood "eating house" or from a company that delivers them to homes by means of underground rail routes. In both arrangements, food professionals do the meal planning, serving, and cleaning up afterward, resulting in a dramatic general increase both in leisure time and in good family health.

The residential blocks of metropolitan areas have now all been built in "associated" groupings around central cloistered gardens. In addition to

Idealized rendering of "Central Court of the Proposed Unified City Block,"
drawn by Vernon Howe Bailey. Gilman featured it in her 1909 *Independent*
article entitled "The Beauty of a Block."

nursery schools located on rooftops, each cluster of buildings has central housekeeping services (such as laundry, cleaning, and maintenance) available for purchase as well as large common rooms built to accommodate all necessary social functions (such as recreation, exercise, meetings, and concerts).

"Westholm Park," a planned community set in a rural landscape not far from New York City, is an important stop on John Robertson's introductory itinerary. Built on 300 acres, it has become a design model for suburban areas throughout the transformed American society. Its residential area consists of thirty detached, single-family homes, each built on about an acre of land, each serviced by a central hotel where another hundred people, singles and small families, live. The food and other domestic services are run out of the hotel. Several acres are set aside for community facilities such as a central utilites plant and a recreation hall equipped with bowling alleys, billiards, and a ballroom. Well-equipped school buildings, playgrounds, and a swimming pool are grouped together in a special children's area. A central guest house removes the necessity for each separate home to have its own guest facilities. The remaining 260 acres are devoted to woodland, pasturage, gardens, and meadows. Since 250 people live here year-round, and numerous others visit for extended periods either in the hotel or the guest house, Gilman portrayed a large number of the permanent adult residents in service jobs, running the community infrastructure. She depicted some as gardeners, some as managers, with others as teachers, food specialists, or dairy workers.

Because the average workday has been so dramatically shortened in utopia, laborers and professional people have been liberated to spend much more time with their families and friends. Visiting Westholm Park, Robertson observes how the men who reside there spend their afternoons.

> We had seen the fathers come home in time for the noon meal. In the afternoon most of the parents seemed to think it the finest thing in the world to watch their children learning or playing together, in that amazing Garden of theirs, or to bring them home for more individual companionship. As a matter of fact, I had never seen, in any group of homes that I could recall, so much time given to children by so many parents—unless on a Sunday in the suburbs.[13]

Looking back on his visit, Robertson muses on how, after lunch, fathers and mothers, boys and girls "sat on broad piazzas, swung in hammocks, played tennis, ball, croquet, tether-ball and badminton," enjoying themselves in a lovely setting.

In keeping with the pronounced affluence of utopia, the buildings used as workplaces both in city and country bear more resemblance to majestic residences than they do to the dingy factories common at the turn of the century. Just past Staten Island at the end of his homeward voyage, Robertson gapes at "banks of palaces" along the Brooklyn shoreline. He is startled to learn that such "quiet, stately . . . wide windowed, garden roofed" structures are actually the manufacturing centers of the new world. On a subsequent voyage up the Hudson, Owen Montrose gives him the following explanation: "Why shouldn't people work in palaces? It doesn't cost any more to make a beautiful building than an ugly one. Remember we are much richer, now—and have plenty of time, and the spirit of beauty is encouraged."[14]

Apart from its aesthetic qualities, workplace design in utopian Manhattan is approached as an integral part of residential planning, showing a mixed-use approach to urban zoning. Thus workers are never physically distant from their children, just as persons at leisure are never physically distant from their places of work. In *Moving the Mountain,* a utopian neighborhood consists of commercial, industrial, and serviced residential structures, built in easy proximity to one another.

Herways and Beewise, California

"Bee Wise," a short story that appeared in the July 1913 *Forerunner,* provides a colorful, succinct word picture of Gilman's evolving conception of utopia. With rich detail, "Bee Wise" tells the story of Jean, a very talented "woman reporter," a character not unlike the author herself. Here Gilman portrayed the ideal world she would like to have found when she lived in California, a world with ample social and architectural supports both for professional and for family life.

In "Bee Wise," Gilman rendered her utopian thought in traditional, albeit dramatic, sermonic form. "Beewise" and "Herways" are planned, interdependent communities on the California coast. Their names were taken from Scripture, specifically the sixth verse of the sixth chapter of the book of Proverbs. Her text for this fictional sermon reads, "Go to the ant, thou sluggard, consider her ways and be wise." Like the ancient Hebrew poet, Gilman held up the lowly ant as an exemplar of virtuous industry.

Gilman created the linked towns of Herways and Beewise to be models of socialized industry. She described them as "a sample town," "a new example to the world," and "a little Eden." She judged that "The remarkable thing about the two towns was that their population consisted very largely of women and more largely of children, but there were men also, who seemed happy enough."

One of the towns is "a tiny sheltered nook" at the edge of the sea; the other is nestled high in a valley beyond the coastal hills. Together they function as an integrated environment, connected to each other physically by a trolley shuttle called Jacob's Ladder. The seaport community, Herways, is a beautiful industrial park using windmills, a solar engine, and hydroelectric power provided by two swift streams plunging down the canyon from the surrounding hills. Beewise, which is built toward the top of the hillsides, is an exclusive residential community, the buildings of which are attractive, constructed of indigenous materials, comfortable, and "sea-shell clean." They consist of kitchenless houses, a guest house, a recreation center known as the "pleasure garden," a sanitarium, "clean wide" food labs, baby gardens, kindergartens, and schools.

Having traveled there to do a newspaper story about the two towns, Jean is so taken with the place she decides to move there. As a contented new member of the planned community, she conducts her newspaper work in Herways while residing in the hills of Beewise.

The paired towns in this story were established "by women—for women—and *children,*" specifically, by a group of "some dozen or twenty" women who had become close friends in college. Known by their professional roles, in lieu of names, a Teacher, Nurse, Minister, Doctor, Statesman, Artist, and Engineer had agreed at the end of their studies to collaborate with their classmate, Margery (alias "the Manager"), on a development scheme of hers. The Manager, who had already proven herself competent in business, had been surprised to learn that her long-lost goldminer great-uncle had decided, as an investment, to give her $10,000,000 worth of land and more liquid assets.

In response to her windfall, Margery had proposed to her friends that they jointly build two perfect, interdependent towns, which could be replicated all over the country. The classmates agreed to her plan, not as a communitarian experiment but as "a plain business offer."

Unlike the Ruskin colony at which Gilman had scoffed due to its lack of "a legitimate local economic base and relationship," Herways and Beewise have a strong, diversified foundation. The utopian economy consists of a "little port on the coast" with shipping, manufacturing, and recreational facilities, as well as a fertile agricultural valley in the hills

Beewise/Herways. 1988 drawing by David Wynn Robinson.

above, where produce and livestock are grown and traditional crafts conducted both for community use and for sale. Electrical power is in bountiful supply throughout.

Not just anybody can come to live in Herways/Beewise. For purposes of assured felicity and eugenics, the community's Manager and her associates adopted strict population-control measures. According to their entrance requirements, "no one could live there without being admitted by the others"; the "prime condition" of admission is a commitment to "social service." Lots of people have been turned down for membership because each has to be "clean physically and morally" as well as active in a type of work needed by the community. The towns have applications from more doctors, dentists, and other professional people than they can accommodate. Most town residents are "more immediately necessary workers," that is, they are the men and women who dig ditches, run machinery, spin, weave, prepare food, care for children, and generally attend "to the daily wants of the community." So that they won't develop "the diseases of cities," the town managers are determined to keep their population density down to "normal limits."

Herland

Herland is an exotic country at an unspecified point somewhere in the Southern Hemisphere, a land inhabited by strong, handsome "Aryan" women and no men. After hearing rumors during their travels of "a strange and terrible 'Woman Land,'" a previously undiscovered "Feminisia" not to be found on conventional maps, three male adventurers from the United States set out to find and explore it.

Engagingly told in the first person by Vandyck ("Van") Jennings, an open-minded, eminently teachable sociologist, *Herland* portrays a nonurban, preindustrial paradise. With his friends Terry Nicholson and Jeff Margrave, Jennings goes, by boat, plane, and foot, up "a dark tangle of rivers, lakes, morasses and dense forests" in search of this intriguing place. At the end of their journey, deep in a range of "mighty mountains," they find a country "about the size of Holland, some ten or twelve thousand square miles," with a population of about three million. With its "clean, well-built roads," its California-style building material dominated by "dull rose-colored stone," its white public buildings and "green groves and gardens," Herland looks to the travelers like one "enormous park."[15]

Upon arriving in Herland, the explorers are startled to find a highly advanced civilization created by these women. They are even more

amazed at the character of the women themselves, at how unlike stereo-
typical American females they are. The women who capture, sedate, and
confine them in a very comfortably appointed wing of "a sort of castle" are
very sure of themselves and wise. They are also physically fit, productive,
and unflirtatious.

The travelers are struck by the fact that their hostesses do not defer to
them but rather treat them exactly as they do one another. Nicholson, the
most incorrigible sexist of the three visitors, complains of missing such
womanly virtues in Herland as modesty, patience, submissiveness, and
"that natural yielding which is woman's greatest charm."[16] Scolding him
for not appreciating the Herlanders *human* virtues, Jennings urges Nicholson to apologize to the women for his pigheadedness. Jennings, the ever-
thoughtful sociologist, does a lot of soul searching about American ways of
keeping women as different from men as possible. After more than a year
in Herland, he reports that "We were now well used to seeing women not
as females, but as people: people of all sorts, doing every kind of work."[17]

During their visit, the men learn about the unusual biological under-
pinnings of this all-female society. Residents of Herland, like certain
insects and plants, have the power to reproduce themselves asexually by
parthenogenesis, that is, without male fertilization. These self-sufficient
women produce girl babies only, who in turn grow to maturity endowed
with the same remarkable reproductive capacity.

Upon inquiring into the origins of this biological anomaly, the men are
told that all of the native males had been destroyed "about two thousand
years ago." This had come about as a result of both natural and historical
events. "Decimated by war," earthquake, and volcano, the few remaining
men had been liquidated during a bold uprising of young women against
their "brutal" oppressors. Shortly after the women's desperate revolt, the
first foremother of Herland had discovered that she possessed the surprising "virgin birth capacity" when she brought forth five daughters. When
these daughters had reached maturity, each of them in turn gave birth to
five daughters herself. After the nation was well established by several
generations of multiple daughters, a quota of "one woman : one child"
was imposed on all but the most exceptional women ("Over-Mothers") in
order to control population growth and enhance the general welfare.[18]

Ellador, the main female character in *Herland,* incarnates perfect human character according to Gilman. As Ellador introduces Jennings to the
wonders of Herland, learning from him in turn about the world beyond its
borders, the two idealists fall in love and agree to be married. In subplots

of lesser significance, Nicholson and Margrave also find romance and persuade their handsome sweethearts to marry them and experiment with heterosexual reproduction.

After a triple wedding ceremony, Quaker-style, the three couples go their separate ways, Margrave and his bride settle happily in Herland. Nicholson abuses his wife with his unreconstructed male-chauvinist manners and is expelled from the country, his marriage revoked. Van and Ellador embark on an extensive journey, which is described in the sequel to *Herland*.

Gilman provided considerably less design detail in her evocation of Herland than she did in her characterizations of revised New York City and Beewise/Herways. Her fantasy country with no men is less a portrait of a physical landscape than it is a depiction of a transformed cultural consciousness. The most striking feature of Herland is its pro-woman spirit, which supports the strong development both of individual women and of sisterly cooperation.

Although Gilman was relatively unspecific about the built form of this utopia, Herland did have several hallmarks of the other mythological places. All its villages, towns, and cities, for example, have the same "parklike beauty." Town centers are built to resemble orderly college campuses. Conveniently located, free gymnasiums greatly enhance the physical fitness of all residents. Eating gardens and eating houses are scattered around the country. Community childcare facilities have been constructed, kibbutz-style, in the warmer part of the country.

With Her in Ourland

In Gilman's last utopian novel, she did not attempt to portray an ideal neighborhood design. She had created Herland more to underscore the righteousness of her perspective than to lay out an alternative blueprint. By 1915 she was no longer motivated to create a detailed vision of buildable landscapes. In both the Herland books, she paid more attention to the requirements of personal comfort (such as two rooms and a bath for every citizen) than she had in the earlier stories.

The story of *With Her in Ourland* follows the extensive, round-the-world travels of newlyweds Van and Ellador. After a brief time in England and western Europe, the sojourners spend time in northern Africa, in Southeast Asia, China, Japan, and Hawaii before actually arriving in the United States. As part of Ellador's "Journey of Inspection," she travels to every state in the United States, studying, observing, and asking questions.

The tirelessness of her travel mission on behalf of progressive social change makes for a mostly tiresome story.

Gilman's central reason for creating Herland was to establish the legitimacy of her architectural and social insight. Ellador, as her auto-biographical projection, is recognized in the United States "as an observer far beyond our best scientists." Her adoring husband states that she is as "dispassionate and impartial as a visiting angel," likening her to a "Martian" or "an Investigating Committee from another world."[19] Gilman thus claimed that the validity of her ideas would be confirmed by the approval of an unbiased party coming into the world from beyond it.

Ellador's sense of mission was a fictional rendering of Gilman's own, with the enhanced authority that comes from being an "extramundane." Van's enthusiasm about it describes Gilman's own educational purpose. "You are the most important ambassador that ever was," he exclaimed. "You are sent from your upland island, your little hidden heaven, to see our poor blind bleeding world and carry news of it to your people. Perhaps that vast storehouse of mother-love can help to set us straight at last." Ellador, like Gilman herself, was on an extended pilgrimage to uplift the world.

GILMAN'S COMPOSITE UTOPIA

Gilman's fictional portraits of utopia provide a revealing look at her perspective on a number of matters. While writing fiction she was not as self-conscious, as concerned with being politically correct as she was when writing social theory. As storyteller, she let down her dogmatic guard a little (more so in her "realistic" than in her "utopian" stories). It is therefore possible to extract her views in a suggestive way by examining the different kinds of institutions she was conjuring up in her imaginary landscapes.

Gilman told quite different utopian stories in 1911 and 1915; and the one she published in 1913 suggests some intriguing things about the direction her thinking was taking during those years. Although several important dimensions of her utopia were changing, there were definite continuities between the stories as well.

Gilman consistently stressed the importance of respect for the natural surroundings of buildings. In many of her concerns, she was an early environmentalist. In each of her utopian places no pollution was tolerated, so that only ecologically sound forms of transportation and energy production were built. As a result, all the rivers, harbors, factories, highways and riverbanks were sparkling clean, the entire ecosystem healthy.

In a similar vein, the population throughout Gilman's utopia looked to plants and nutbearing trees rather than to animals as primary sources of protein. Her predilection for vegetarianism arose both from her commitment to democratic nutritional access and from her belief that meatless meals were decidedly healthier. Her reverent concern for the preservation of soil and seed led her to dwell at some length on the virtues of "chestnut, walnut, butternut, [and] pecan" trees as precious resources for the provision of plentiful, economical food.

Gilman regularly described a contiguous mix of residences and workplaces in her imaginary environments. Her fictional designers and builders saw to it that users could enjoy ease of movement, back and forth, between home and work. She envisioned a world in which industrial and commercial buildings are connected with residences by direct, modern transportation systems. Clustered around parks and open spaces, the proximity of housing to workplace and childcare centers in utopia allows parents of young children, even nursing mothers, to commute easily by foot between their several responsibilites.

The most noteworthy shifts in Gilman's utopian thought can be seen in two places: first, in the degree of urbanism in the several settings of the stories; second, in the family life styles of the three sets of characters. In *Moving the Mountain,* the panorama of Gilman's imagination is the widest; it includes by far the most well-defined urban environment, as well as a detailed look at a suburban design. Gilman described in detail the bisection and beautification of city blocks into parks and patios. She provided facts and figures concerning salaries and job benefits associated with the new food service. She discussed plans drawn up by women architects for both social, communal living space and private, family living space, plans that had been implemented citywide. These liberated environments included nursery schools and kindergardens on urban rooftops or in special buildings in Westholm Park.

In contrast, the representation of utopia in Herland is much more rustic. Its unspoiled, rural ambience has a nostalgic quality that is decidedly premodern. In her final myth, Gilman had lost interest in describing the built environment. Although Herlanders mostly live in villages, the reader has to look long and hard for hints about how those villages look. Particulars of domestic architecture are absent. Instead of a bold imagination of the future, Herland can be read as a lament for a bygone, preindustrial simplicity.

"Bee Wise" is midway between the first and third utopian stories, both in design detail and in its date of publication. Along the California coast, the tandem towns of Beewise and Herways have an agreeable mixture of urban and rural aspects. Their linkage of an exemplary industrial park with serviced residences is actually a prototype for an ideal suburban development.

Even more pronounced than Gilman's dwindling concern with the architecture of cities was the changing composition of her casts of characters. In *Moving the Mountain,* the inhabitants of Gilman's transformed environment are traditional families, men, women, and children, equally enjoying the amenities of utopia. John Robertson is the protagonist. In Beewise/Herways, although there are some traditional marriages in the towns, most of the residents are women and children. Along with her friends, the town mothers, the protagonist of this story is the woman reporter named Jean. When we come to Herland, there are no men at all. Besides losing interest in the details of design during this period, Gilman was becoming both less hopeful about the prospects for traditional families and more positive about the necessity for all-women spaces in the struggle for genuine liberation.

Although she wanted everyone to be able to live in utopian circumstances, Gilman tended to concentrate in her stories on the experience of the well-to-do. The two main characters in *Moving the Mountain,* for example, think nothing of taking a trans-Atlantic cruise. With private property in Herland deemed as passe as "feudalism," Van and Ellador can still afford to spend a year flying around the world. Gilman invested the professional women in Beewise/Herways with more individuality than she gave the people who do the housekeeping work. Although she liked to think that there would always be plenty of wealth to go around, it's hard to miss the probability that only rich people could afford to live in Gilman's utopia.

Worst of all, Gilman envisioned a starkly racist utopia with sternly repressive policies. The inhabitants of Herland, for example, are not only all women; they are all "Aryan" women. They may have admirable ways of cooperating in their child care, but they also apply insidious standards to determine who will bear children. In the other stories as well, Gilman sometimes seemed as concerned that the human species be perfected biologically as she was that it be socially democratic. In her vision of New York City, "hopeless degenerates" and idiots have been "mercifully" done away with, that is to say, killed.[20] In addition, a policy of forced sterilization is applied to certain types of "defectives and degenerates . . . criminals and perverts."[21] Gilman's egalitarian social values were seriously tainted by her racist enthusiasm for biological integrity.

It is interesting to note that only six years before she walked out of Heterodoxy in an antipacifist protest, Gilman was calling for no military budget in her progressive world in order to fund basic human needs. Her utopian world had other positive features. There she was able to discuss, in a suggestive, indirect way, issues of communal child care, public transportation, shorter workdays, food supply, housing design, and other matters of concern to contemporary feminists. Although there were disappointing lapses in her democratic vision, her utopian imagination added important dramatic dimensions to her architectural feminism.

CHAPTER FIVE

Gilman's Pragmatic Approach to Neighborhood Design

"That's her life. It was my mother's too. Always fussing and
fussing. Their houses on their backs—like snails!"

Diantha went all over the place, inch by inch, her eyes widening
with admiration. . . . her professional soul blazed with enthusiasm
over the great kitchens, clean as a hospital, glittering in glass and
copper and cool tiling, with the swift, sure electric stoves.

What Diantha Did
chapters five and fourteen

Gilman addressing a public gathering at Union Square in New York City,
about 1910.

NEW MEDIA FOR A FEMINIST/SOCIALIST MESSAGE

It would be difficult to name a medium that Gilman did not employ to convey the urgency of spatial reformation. She spoke, drew, sang, wrote, clowned, threatened, and cajoled her contemporaries to persuade them of the environmental possibilities of modernity.

Two particularly impressive techniques, which she employed for several decades, involved her writing skills. In the first instance, she wrote a stream of short, detailed articles advocating socialized homes. Both in California and New York, she succeeded in placing these pieces in the mainstream, commerical press as well as in smaller political journals. Quite frequently she illustrated her magazine articles graphically, using design sketches as well as photographs showing extant buildings that she liked.

Gilman's other notable writing technique involved a more down-to-earth style of storytelling than her utopian one. Although many of her realistic tales advocated architectural change in subtle, oblique ways, one in particular, *What Diantha Did,* was just about as didactic as it could be. And yet, attesting to her flair for fiction, it is, nonetheless, an engaging, entertaining story.

This chapter sets forth Gilman's most noteworthy efforts to address practical aspects of socialized neighborhood design. After looking at her straightforward journalistic arguments as well as *What Diantha Did,* it will consider the means by which she expected the built environment to change.

DISCUSSING DESIGN SPECIFICATIONS IN POPULAR MAGAZINES AND NEWSPAPERS

In addition to her books and her own monthly magazine, Gilman spelled out her architectural vision in dozens of articles published in magazines and papers with mass circulation. Here, attempting to capture the imagination of urban planners, developers, and builders, as well as potential consumers, she painstakingly addressed practical questions of design and cost. Recognizing the accelerating pressures in cities for decent, affordable housing, she aimed to exert an influence both on the building of new neighborhoods and on the renovation of older ones.

Gilman proposed that the apartment hotel be taken as a model and adapted to the distinctive character of particular localities. In her most widely read book, she had described the main features of such a building.

> The apartments would be without kitchens; but there would be a kitchen belonging to the house from which meals could be served to the families in their rooms or in a common dining-room, as preferred. It would be a home where the cleaning was done by efficient workers, not hired separately by the families, but engaged by the manager of the establishment; and a roof-garden, day nursery, and kindergarten, under well-trained professional nurses and teachers, would insure proper care of the children.[1]

Although, in her day, such dwellings were affordable only by the very wealthy, Gilman appealed to right-thinking developers to see to it that the model was democratized and mass-produced.

> As a matter of fact we have now all the main features of these new forms of living in our expensive apartment hotels. The same essentials, and some others, can be furnished at much less expense, as soon as far-seeing builders recognize the demand.
>
> Much useless splendor in decoration could be spared, much ostentation of liveried service; but the great saving comes in making one kitchen in place of five hundred, and providing properly prepared, simple food for a regular patronage in place of the lavish and wasteful catering of the costly restaurant or cafe.[2]

In an impressively detailed article first published in the *New York Evening Post,* Gilman told builders that they had a civic obligation to construct socialized housing for low-income families. She chided profit-minded developers (whom she called "house farmers") for laboring "under the economic delusion that a house was a species of rent-cow, a thing to be milked for money."

Arguing the advantages to working people of shared residential facilities, Gilman instructed present and prospective owners of rental property that they "should give, in return for their rent, a full measure of value in human living." She encouraged the conscientious builder to incorporate certain minimal specifications into every dwelling constructed: "first, to allow room for proper care of children; second, to allow room for amusement and association; third, to allow of such service as shall reduce living expenses and enable the woman to earn her share of the income, thus nearly doubling it. The last proviso means an arrangement for large food laboratories." Addressing the minute particulars of cost, floor plan, staffing, and the multiple uses of social spaces, Gilman insisted that, especially where the poor were concerned, adequate social facilities should be considered basic necessities. "Space for amusement and association," she wrote, "means that the builder of houses should recognize that these are human needs, that they must be met; and that they are better met when given to the families in the house, than when sought by individuals in the street." Because of the density of population in working-class neighborhoods, Gilman anticipated that the average low-income residential development would require "six kitchens to a block."[3]

Gilman's choice of art work enhanced her arguments for socialized environments. In a lively and appealing article entitled "The Beauty of the Block," she furnished diagrams showing the "front elevation" and "ground plan" of a typical New York City residential block as well as the alternative block design she was promoting. She expressed contempt for the so-called homes available in blocks built according to "Present-Day Individualistic Construction." "All these huddled houses, pressed into a solid cubical honeycomb (without the honey!)," she wrote, "stand presenting their shrunken and wasted rears to one another, while the denizens have no outlook of beauty in any direction."[4]

To correct the "grinding monotony, unbroken ugliness, and crowding" characteristic of such architecture, Gilman proposed the "Unified Construction of a City Block." She contended that making the open yard space in the center of a city block "a place to dry clothes!" was patently absurd; she argued that "a better wisdom will have all such work done in the clean, windy, open country—it does not belong in the city nor at home."[5] She liked to speak of all the improvements that could be provided, once private utility spaces were rendered obsolete.

> The yard space could become an exquisite little park, a court, with vines and fountains, with delicious oriel windows, balconies, shaded corners, shrubs and flowers. Or tennis courts could be laid out, and tether ball poles set up; there is room for a good deal of pleasure in 12,500 square feet.
>
> Around the whole basement story a pillared cloister could run, the top of which would form a separate balcony space for each family, from which a little stair would give entrance to the court.

Contrasting designs illustrating strictly autonomous, redundant planning and the more progressive, integrated approach that Gilman advocated. She included these two photographs in "The Beauty of a Block," 1909.

Openings to the street would make this court cool and breezy, yet these could be closed in winter and keep [*sic*] it sheltered, and barred at all times from intrusion.

This place would be to the tenants what those elegant and select fenced gardens in little squares are to London residents, each paying for his share of its privilege in his rent. The children's playground would be, best of all, on the roof, and larger than the court; but this would give a central spot of beauty, of air and exercise, to the older occupants.[6]

Gilman was quick to point out how cellar and basement floors could be used more creatively and efficiently. In her domestic blueprints, she usually placed food laboratories and athletic and social facilities on the lower levels. She had an extensive architectural dream list, which she liked to embellish with fictional rhetoric, as in this cameo scene:

"Our club has all the home comforts," said the man in the story. "Yes," replied his wife, "and when will our home have all the club comforts?"

When we build them into each block. When we recognize the swimming pool and gymnasium as common comforts and necessities of life. When we have billiards and bowling and all manner of easy games, shorn of artificial and dangerous allurements, and handy for mother as well as father.

When the well stocked reading-room furnishes papers and magazines to every one, and the music-room, dancing-room and lecture-room make possible all manner of pleasant association as a common custom of civilized living. All these things are now provided in our magnificent apartment houses with their magnificent prices. They could be provided to every family in an average block, and within the same rents now paid for the sacredly vertical bunch of rooms and the unspeakably holy back-yard.[7]

In addition to her conception of how city neighborhoods should look, Gilman gave consideration as well to the design of suburbs, small towns, and rural areas. She felt, in general, that there would appropriately be so much variation from one locale to another that she could not foresee in detail how different communities would look. But she assumed that they would each be served by a "food supply company" of some sort. Going out from the central cities, she recommended "a grouping of adjacent houses, each distinct and having its own yard, but all kitchenless, and connected by covered ways with the eating-house."[8] In the case of farm villages, she suggested that pie-shaped farms be clustered around a community center equipped with all sorts of social conveniences and enhancements. In that way, farmhouses, built in a circle near the village center, would be readily accessible both to each other and to centrally provided household services instead of randomly scattered and isolated. She proposed that cultivated farmlands stretch out behind each home in triangular fashion, thereby fostering maximal collaboration, equality, and productivity among farming men and women.[9]

Because Gilman saw the private kitchen as the root of the problem in conventional neighborhoods, she went into the most detail when describing her proposed facilities for the daily provision of cooked food. In her design, commerical "cookshops" would replace individual kitchens, in villages, towns, and cities. Highly skilled workers in clean, economical, efficient "distributing kitchens" would plan, prepare, and serve the most delicious, nutritionally sound, economical meals imaginable. Large dining rooms would be built in urban apartment buildings, providing each client or client-family with its own table. "Eating houses" serving several detached households would contain kitchen and dining facilities for individuals and families within a certain radius in a given neighborhood. Fleets of delivery wagons or overhead trolleys would deliver cooked food in areas where a common building was not feasible. Also, when apartment or house dwellers preferred to dine in their own homes, dumbwaiters or van trucks would deliver piping hot food to them in " 'thermos'-like containers" and return later to remove the soiled dinnerware.

Gilman amassed pages and pages of calculations to demonstrate the wasteful expenditures involved in maintaining detached kitchens. With long columns of comparative cost figures, she illustrated the fiscal saving to be realized by adopting her "organized industry" plan of food processing.[10] She maintained that the organized industry method would afford its clients "the maximum of nutrition and healthy pleasure, with the minimum of effort and expense." As exemplars of the preferred system she cited the "flourishing" business enjoyed by cooked food supply companies in New Haven, Connecticut, Pittsburgh, Pennsylvania, Boston, Massachusetts, and Montclair, New Jersey.[11] To demonstrate the feasibility of adapting her food-delivery ideas for the least affluent, she described "The flourishing Boston restaurant, where people sit about ring tables, and the food comes up in the middle from the kitchen below," claiming that it

Diagram showing advantages of cluster zoning in rural areas. It would simultaneously enhance social access, efficiency, and land conservation. Artist unspecified. Drawing of village resembles cross-section of grapefruit with pie-shaped farms surrounding it. From a Gilman article entitled "Applepieville," published in *The Independent,* September 25, 1920.

"shows us a simple way of avoiding waiters, and the dinner pails could be packed to order while the breakfast was being eaten."[12]

Gilman expected the centralized kitchens of the future to employ "about eight percent of the adult population." She anticipated that providing quality cooked food would be "a large and important trade" for well-paid professionals.[13] She claimed that a small staff of competent "food specialists" working in a well-designed kitchen would be able easily to execute the work that hundreds of individuals in their separate kitchens were presently struggling in vain to accomplish. Transferring responsibility for meals to professionals, she pointed out, would liberate rank-and-file women from "the compulsion of preparing ten hundred and ninety five meals in a year."[14]

Gilman insisted that patrons of cookshops would be able to purchase their food from a wide variety of menus sure to include their personal favorites. "Each family," she reasoned, "could order with the same freedom it does now, only instead of ordering its food raw, from butcher, grocer, baker, confectioner, fishman, iceman, milkman, and fruiterer, it would order of one shop—and receive it ready to eat." She summed up the proposed system's advantages succinctly. "This is the essence of the change in a nutshell. We are going to buy food, cooked food, instead of raw materials."[15]

The provision of comprehensive community childcare in every neighborhood was a constant element in Gilman's practical as well as her utopian writings. Although she went into much less fiscal and physical detail about nurseries than she did about large-scale kitchens, she wrote numerous articles (and an entire book, *Concerning Children*) to establish the principle that children, "our most important citizens," should be educated with reverence in perfectly appointed spaces. Youngsters were entitled, she argued, from infancy forward, to a well-equipped, professionally staffed, positively attractive place of their own.

On a societywide basis, Gilman estimated that an ideal ratio of facilities to patrons would provide one child-care center for every twenty to thirty families.[16] She proposed that a "child home" with appropriate environments for each age group be built in every neighborhood save in the most isolated rural areas.

Gilman said a lot more about how rooms for infants should look than she did about her plans for school-age children and teenagers. According to her specifications, the "special house for children" would accommodate babies in "cornerless rooms, the curved, hurt-proof walls of which

A large, commercial-style kitchen serving a central dining room, crucial to
Gilman's architectural program. Published as part of article by Gilman,
"The Passing of the Home in Great American Cities," in *Cosmopolitan,*
December 1904.

would be padded and furnished with cushioned, built-in benches." In areas provided for toddlers, she envisioned that

> Large soft ropes, running across here and there, within reach of the eager, strong little hands, would strengthen arms and chest, and help in walking. A shallow pool of water, heated to suitable temperature, with the careful trainer always at hand, would delight, occupy, and educate for daily hours. A place of clean, warm sand, another of clay, with a few simple tools,—these four things— water, sand, clay, and ropes to climb on—would fill the days of happy little children without further toys.[17]

Gilman's favorite image of a child-care center was "the big bright baby garden on the roof."[18] She expected that the construction of child gardens in large urban areas would prove relatively simple. This was because she thought that families living in such close proximity to each other would instantly grasp the rightness of collective solutions to their child-rearing problems. She confidently expected that thousands of centers, each "beautiful, comfortable, hygienic, safe and sweet and near," would soon be operating throughout the land.[19]

WHAT DIANTHA DID

Gilman set forth the commercial apparatus she had in mind for the domestic industries very forcefully in a novel published in the *Forerunner* during its first year. *What Diantha Did* is a memorable tale about Diantha Bell, an aspiring young woman who establishes a highly successful house-keeping business in Orchardina, California. Frustrated both by her economic dependence on men and the narrowness of conventional expectations about women's roles, the heroine stops teaching in order to start a business, expecting it to be both a financial "gold mine" and an indispensable public service.

Everyone in her family (as well as her fiancé) is appalled when Bell takes a position as a domestic servant in the first phase of her business venture. She chooses to work for Isabel Porne, a talented architect whose newly acquired family responsibilities are driving her to distraction. Having drawn up a very professional contract stating exactly what regular duties she would and would not perform for six months, Bell manages the Porne household with such consummate skill and grace that the whole town is soon singing her praises. During the last three of her months there, she also convenes a weekly "girls' club" in the Porne kitchen, there instructing "poor," "ignorant" young women both in dressmaking and "in easy and thorough methods of housework."

Bell extends her educational work by accepting an invitation from the "Home and Culture Club" of Orchardina to address them on the topic, "The True Nature of Domestic Industry." Here she presents, eloquently and succinctly, her vision of kitchenless households that employ skilled labor by the hour. Feelings in the audience run high, both among those who perceive Diantha as a prophet of a fairer day and among others who regard her program as foolish, dangerous, and heretical. Antagonism between the two groups is so intense that the Bell enthusiasts secede from the old club and establish thier own "New Women's Club of Orchardina."

With the financial backing of Viva Weatherstone, a wealthy young widow in the breakaway club, Bell organizes a housekeeping shop called Union House, out of which are run a laundry, a cooked food service, a cleaning service, and, later, a restaurant. Business is so brisk that people in eighteen other cities establish imitation enterprises. With the architectural cooperation of Isabel Porne, Bell and Watherstone develop an entire neighborhood, which they call Hotel del las Casas. This development features a large hotel with both a central eating facility and all manner of indoor and outdoor social spaces. Twenty small, "unostentatious" houses are clustered around the hotel, each "nestled" in its own "hedged garden," with a community playground and nursery located picturesquely in one corner.

By the end of the story, not only has Diantha Bell done what she set out to do with stunning success. In addition, the most important members of her family (and her fiancé) have come to esteem her work and admire her pluck. Her mother, now employed by Bell's business as a bookkeeper, is enjoying the first real job satisfaction of her life. Her father, having retired, is now permanently, blissfully, residing in his daughter's hotel. And her long-skeptical fiancé (now her husband) has been converted to a deep respect for her pioneering efforts to socialize housework. No longer chagrined by her unusual sense of calling, he becomes "tremendously proud" of her. And the two of them, with three babies, and an equal importance attached to each of their work, live happily ever after.

GILMAN'S STRATEGY FOR CHANGING THE BUILT ENVIRONMENT

Gilman was not clear about the extent of social reorganization necessary to implement her proposals. On the one hand, she often claimed that socialized housekeeping would cost substantially less in dollars, not only to participating clients but also to society as a whole, thus enhancing everyone's spending power in other areas. In such instances, the only fundamental change she anticipated was a dramatic increase in capitalist efficiency.

On the other hand, Gilman sometimes confidently predicted a dramatic, full-fledged social revolution. She anticipated a process by which American society would slough off capitalism like a dead skin to make way for a more adaptive, modern, socialist system. At such moments, she looked forward to extensive changes in all the structures of society as a necessary part of domestic revolution.

Gilman's expectations concerning the economic footing for her program were thus both vague and vacillating. She expressed the more sweeping socialist assumptions in *Moving the Mountain* and *Herland*. In the earlier novel, she implied that a societywide conversion to socialism must needs precede the residential revisions for which she campaigned. Before he could correctly comprehend the particulars of change in Manhattan, for example, John Robertson had to grasp the new economic spirit that had been established there. According to his brother-in-law's explanation, society was now organized according to "real socialism," by which he meant that "The wealth and power of all of us belongs to all of us now. The Wolf is dead."[20] In the second Herland novel, Ellador, prescribing for the social ills of the United States, told Americans that they should adopt a centrally controlled economy, the public ownership of all major industries and natural resources, and a guaranteed annual income for all citizens, imitating her exemplary state.[21]

In her practical writings, Gilman concentrated on increasing the efficiency of capitalist institutions. Forgetting her utopian pronouncements about the superiority of socialist to capitalist organization, she here became positively euphoric about the lucrative possibilities in specialized housework. She was convinced that the thousands of modern families whose adult female members wanted and/or needed to work outside the home constituted a vast and rapidly growing market for commercial domesticity. She often pointed out the cost saving that could be had by purchasing equipment and raw materials in wholesale instead of retail quantities. Noting both the sturdy market for her scheme and its impressive economies of scale, she maintained that handsome profits could be made in such businesses.

Gilman saw no contradiction between socialist ideals and capitalist practice. She favored a mixed economy, a reformed, humanitarian brand of state capitalism. She portrayed her new housekeeping services as privately owned, lucrative businesses, softened sometimes by profit sharing. The wholesale introduction of socialist ideas into American society was her strategy for modifying capitalism.

As far as Gilman was concerned, the verdict was still out on capitalism. She intended to try to reform it before concluding that a distinctly different system was necessary. As a challenge to the hypothesis that socialism was the only humane economic system, she proposed that businesses revise themselves democratically. If privately owned companies would only stop exploiting people and reorganize themselves ethically, she reasoned, there would be nothing morally wrong with their realizing steady profits. In place of greed, she suggested, employers should cultivate a generous contentment with the satisfactions of vital productivity, a contentment to be expressed in fair shares for workers, owners, and consumers alike. When such reforms had been effected, she believed, society would enjoy a harmonious blend of socialist values and capitalist institutions.

Gilman had a diffuse sense that the state could and would promote more democratic dwellings. Like Bellamy and Ward, she believed that the government should be a benign agency of general social amelioration. She did not concern herself with the specifics of legislation or elections or government policies. Living most of her life without the vote, she looked to more informal means to implement her proposals.

Gilman's hopes lay in persuading people to take action. To that educational, moralistic end, she described model places—poetically and practically—to evoke positive feelings about environmental change. Beewise/Herways were exemplary towns, designed to inspire imitation. Diantha's Union House had the same purpose, as did the unified urban buildings described in great detail in her popular articles.

With her lack of political sophistication and her positive sympathy for the capitalist spirit, one of Gilman's preferred strategies was to win the favor of wealthy individuals. She aimed to influence them to put their money to work in building socialized neighborhoods. Many of her stories have this theme, as illustrated by the gold miner in "Bee Wise" with $10,000,000 and Viva Weatherstone in *Diantha* with countless thousands of dollars to invest in constructing progressive spaces. Gilman identified with the owners in American society. As she saw it, people with money could make things happen. She appealed to the affluent on grounds of both altruism and self-interest, urging them to undertake the physical building of an alternative communal environment.

CHAPTER SIX

Gilman's Philosophy of World Improvement Led by Women

Oh, we who are one body of one soul!
Great soul of man born into social form!
Should we not suffer at dismemberment?
A finger torn from brotherhood; an eye
Having no cause to see when set alone.
　　　Our separation is the agony
Of uses unfulfilled—of thwarted law;
The forces of all nature throb and push,
　Crying for their accustomed avenues;
And we, alone, have no excuse to be,—
　No reason for our being. We are dead
Before we die, and know it in our hearts.

. . . .
　　　When we shall learn
　To live together fully; when each man
And woman works in conscious interchange
With all the world,—union as wide as man,—
　No human soul can ever suffer more
　The devastating grief of loneliness.

"Our Loneliness"
CHARLOTTE PERKINS STETSON

Gilman had a philosophical strategy as well as an architectural one for winning equality for women and economic democracy for society as a whole. Driven by an integrative impulse to discuss the human condition exhaustively, she turned, over and over again, from the challenge of actually collectivizing neighborhoods to the expression of her intuitive theology of social unity. It contained the enthusiastic illusions of much progressive thought concerning the impending establishment of socialism in America. It proceeded from a sense of malaise about the exploitation of workers by capitalists, confident that the beneficent motion of social evolution would soon improve the situation. Whereas her feminism proceeded from a detailed empirical analysis of the conventional home, her philosophy of world improvement began with several abstract ideas to which she was deeply committed.

In creating her comprehensive moral theory, Gilman fashioned an idealistic grid, which she held up to recalcitrant social reality, hoping to inspire her readers to more altruistic, less selfish behavior. This chapter examines the three main ideas that constituted that grid; they were formative of her approach to theory building.

The first idea celebrated the social unity of the human species, claiming that social life is actually more sacred than individual life; Gilman believed that the widespread recognition of organic human relatedness would be an important prerequisite for the development of a modern social morality adequate to guide industrial society. The second idea so elevated human goodness and evolutionary progress that it denied the presence of evil in the world; the only thing wrong with the world, she argued, was that people were clinging to false, antiquated concepts. The third idea bestowed upon women the dubious honor of being the more altruistic sex; it maintained that women were uniquely endowed by nature with greater capacities than men for nurturance, industry, and service. After examining the origins of each of these notions in turn, and their interdependence, the chapter will conclude by discussing both the intellectual trap which they became for Gilman and the inherent futility of "doing" theory apart from historical engagement.

SOCIAL UNITY AS THE FOUNDATION FOR SOCIAL ETHICS

Charlotte Gilman's fondest ambition was to construct an inclusive system of social morality to replace domestic, "ultrapersonal" morality. Trained as she was to revere socially consecrated intellectual work, she imagined that she could best discredit the ideology of separate gender spheres by persuading people, once and for all, that they lived in one, indivisible moral universe.

In place of a dualistic code of ethics with distinctive duties and virtues according to gender, Gilman aspired to articulate human duties in a timeless, ungendered idiom. "The collapse of the arbitrary and unjust domestic morality of the past," she wrote, "will presently be followed by recognition of the social morality of the future. Rightly discarding artificial standards of virtue based on the pleasure of men, we shall establish new ones based on natural law."[1] The hopeful seriousness with which she approached this task arose from her conviction that the new morality would be based on indisputable facts established by the science of sociology. She was convinced that an unbiased visitor from another planet would instantly recognize the objective validity of the new social standards.

Gilman believed that if she could demonstrate conclusively that everyone had an immediate, compelling stake in the welfare of society as a whole, she would have paved the way for the establishment of both gender equality and economic democracy. Writing in 1898, she maintained that "To desire good things for oneself is selfishness. To desire good things for some one else is unselfishness. To desire good things for all is justice."[2] From her days in the Nationalist and Fabian movements to her retirement days in Norwich Town, Gilman tried to foster a sense of "we-ness" and "our-ness" in place of such primitive notions as "I" and "mine."

To convey a vivid sense of human connectedness, Gilman preached a doctrine of organic social unity that was extremely popular at the turn of the century among socialists, academics, and Social Gospel Christians. The metaphorical use of a biological organism to represent human society had a venerable history dating back to ancient Greece and Israel. Inspired by developments in the fields of biology and evolutionary science, nineteenth-century writers frequently drew such analogies, sometimes claiming, as Gilman often did, that the *only* proper way to comprehend social reality was to view it as a living being.

The major contention of organicist social theories has been that society has a sacrosanct life of its own, which is not to be equated with the mere sum total of its individual members. A society's systems of production, distribution, and government are its organs and life systems. Whereas social contract theories maintain that the human individual is independent of society and endowed with inalienable natural rights, organicist theories tend to demote the individual from an autonomous to a derivative position, arguing that a human being is complete only when understood as an integral part of the social whole.

Originally trained as a biologist, Herbert Spencer forcefully employed the method of organic analogy and analysis in his social theory. In her early reading, Gilman had found Spencer's organicist formulations inspiringly convincing. In her autobiography she noted, "From Spencer I learned wisdom and applied it."[3] Following her mentor, she liked to portray society as a natural being with numerous features in common with a living thing. As the cell was to a plant or animal organism, she reasoned, so was the individual person related to the whole of society.

Assuming that the inviolability of individual rights could serenely be taken for granted and that women could tell that they should develop their individuality, Gilman overstated the organic analogy and thereby robbed individual rights of a secure foundation. In her theoretical mode, she suggested that the flourishing of the social body was of utmost significance whereas the faltering of individual humans, mere cells, could be dismissed as both natural and ultimately beneficial.

In a lifelong stream of books, Gilman tried to foster an awareness of organic unity among all society's peoples, a vital sense of the whole as the primary theater of moral action.[4] As one whom conventional wisdom had assigned to a lesser, separate moral sphere, she was zealous to teach this higher law. She borrowed from J. G. Phelps Stokes the notion of "omniism," which she described as "a feeling for all of us which *includes* the ego." She believed that the spirit of omniism would become so strong and pervasive as to make altruism obsolete. Omniism, she wrote, is "an extension of self-consciousness, a recognition that my self is society, and my 'ego' only a minute fraction of the real me."[5] Her belief in social solidarity had a decidedly mystical quality, inspiring her to evangelical efforts on behalf of its recognition.

Gilman was repudiating "individualism" as a form of consciousness at the same time that she was espousing social organicism. As theorist, she felt the need to choose definitively between individualism and collectivism as the basis for her social ethics. From today's perspective, her conviction that she was involved in an either/or situation appears both quaint and false. She often portrayed "individual" and "social" ethics as mutually exclusive, posing such dilemmas as "whether humanity consists of individuals, or of groups; whether we live and grow individually or socially; whether ethics is to be predicated of individual conduct or of group conduct."[6] In her view, individualism was synonomous with selfishness

1897-

Jan.	15th.	Rochester N.Y.	Unit.Ch.	Collective Ethics .	15.15
''	18th.	''	Soc.L.U.	American Soc.	
''	21st.	Chicago.	Parlor (?)	What We Need to etc.	
''	22nd.	''	Mrs.Coonley's	Gen'l talk.	
''	24th.	''	Mrs.Park's	on The Fabian Soc.	
''	27th.	Des Moines,Ia.	W.S.Conv.	read and Speak .	
''	28th.	'8	''	Duty and Honor .	
''	29th.	''	Address two colleges and Unity Club		
''	31st.	'' Unit.Ch.A.M., Cong.Ch. P.M.		for the two	15.00
Feb.	1st.	Omaha.	Womans Club.	W.& Pol. (cost $9!)	10.00
''	2nd.	D.Moines	H.Pk. Cell.	Our Brains etc.	25.00
(a.m.,inv.of Rep.Bird,I "open with prayer" in House of Rep.)					
'' Chica	8th.	speak at Mrs. Gross'& at Mrs. Coonley's		of Mrs.G.	10.00
''	9th.	another parlor talk,Things we need to know today.			15.00
''	11th.	'' ''	Our Brains etc. (ex.)		15.00
''	12th.	Dowagiac,Mich.	W.Club. The Home, Past, Pres.& Fu.		10.00
''	16th.	Wash. D.C.	W.S.A.	Our Brains etc.	25.00
''	18th.	''	High School	Self Training .	
'8	19th.	''	Natl. Pk. Acad.	Work for Women .	10.00
''	22nd.	New York.	Sunrise Club.	Open Discuss.on Home .	
Mch.	4th.	''	W.S.League.		
''	10th.	Bkln.	Photoreene Reading Cl.	What We Need to	10.00
''	12th.	N.Y.	Man. Lib. Club.	Econ. Basis of W. Q.	10.00
''	20th.	''	Sing.Tax Club.	Why we Work .	
Apl.	1st.	Newark,N.J.	parlor, Mrs. Van Winkle .		10.00
''	11th.	Bkln.	Bkln. Philosoph.Assn.	Econ.B.of W.Q.	5.00
''	12th.	Wilmington.Del.	New Century Cl. The Club Conscien		12.00
''	''	Chester,Pa.	Mrs.Flintcraft's,Social Economics.		5.00
''	13th.	Lansdowne,Pa.	W.S.Co.Assn. America's Place Today.		14.00
''	15th.	Wilmington.	Unit.Ch.		8.00
''	21st.	Harrisburg Pa.	Legislative Chambers, on Woman S.		25.00
''	26th.	Detroit.Mich.	P.A.for W?&C. Society & the Child.		25.00
''	30th.	Savanna Ill.	Things We Need to Know Today.		15.00
May.	2nd.	Keokuk Ia.(?) Unit. Ch.	Heroes we need New.		
''	16th.	Milwaukee.Wis.	Eth.Assn. '' ' '' '		25.00
''	18th.	Chicago.	at Mrs. Parkers. Body, Dress, House.		5.00
''	25th.	Dowagiac.Mich	'' ''	Our Brains .	10.00
''	27th.	'' '' ''		The New Motherhood.	
''	29th.	Battle Creek ''.	W.League. The Power Behind Throne		10.00
''	30th.	''	'' speak at sanitarium & preach evng.(gift)		10.00
2'	31st.	Charlotte Mich.	W. Club I guess, Our Brains		5.00
Jun.	1st.	Kalamazoo ''	W.Cl.	Duties Domestic & Other	15.00
''	10th.	Mankato ?	? Teacher8s Inst.	Our Brains .	25.00
'2	13th.	Topeka,Kan.	Unit. Sh. The Heroes We Etc.		5.00
''	17th.	Eureka ''	Garden Party, Amer.Pl.Today	10.00	10.00
'' n	27th.	''(?)	Cong.Ch. on Social Settlements		3.96/
Jul.	6th.	''	Morning parlor meeting Motherhoodetc.		3.25
''	9th.	Eldorado ''	pm.talk	Public Ownership .	
''	18th.	Wyoming N.Y.	Parlor talk a.m. preach in churchievn.		
''	25th.	Rochester N.Y.	Dr.Gannet's chapel God's Will, head		
Aug.	13th.	St. Hubert's Inn, Adirondacks.	Soc.Organism.(Mr.White		50.00
''	26th.	Greenacre.Me.	at Miss Farmer's, Soc. Organism.		16.50
Oct.	30th.	Wilmington Del.	E 8 Club.		7.00
''	31st	'' ''	Unit.Ch.		10.00

(handwritten notations at bottom:) 5$, 4 1 more - 59 in 97

(handwritten figures, lower right:)
25.55
22.50
10.00
7500

Copy of hand-typed itinerary from Gilman's travels in 1897 demonstrating some of the great variety of her appearances, along with notations of honoraria received.

and part of the obsolete, competitive economic order that was being progressively replaced by cooperative collectivism.

These emphases were not original to Gilman. As a matter of fact, many progressive thinkers were renouncing individualism as a perverse doctrine that was seriously obstructing social evolution. In their view it was time for "individual rights" as an ethical prism to give way to the motif of "social cohesion." In 1909 Charles Eliot, president emeritus of Harvard, portrayed these two conceptions as heroic gladiators on the battlefield of history.

> All through the nineteenth century a conflict was going on in all civilized nations between two opposite tendencies in human society, individualism and collectivism. Till about 1870 individualism had the advantage in this conflict; but near the middle of the century collectivism began to gain on individualism, and during the last third of the century collectivism won decided advantages over the opposing principle.[7]

As odd as it seems today, Gilman and a great many of her progressive colleagues were convinced that enormous moral import rested on one's choice of metaphor for human life.

Gilman got carried away by her enthusiasm for social solidarity. Not only did she give individuals no handle with which to enter her theoretical constructs, stating that the "ego concept" was "pre-human," individualism "an absurdity."[8] Insisting that public interests were of greater importance than individual rights, she condoned eugenicist policies such as sterilizing the "unfit," claiming that such a policy nobly served the general welfare.[9] Her failure to see that an absolute protection of individual rights was a fundamental necessity in any democratic system of social ethics made her theoretical work both incomplete and dangerous.

Gilman was deeply threatened by ideas and impulses she perceived as subversive of universalism. Class, race, and ethnicity had no place in her theoretical ethics. Based on her negative experiences of marginality in a male-centered culture, she sustained an intense determination to protect her metaphysical sense of being connected to the social body.

In celebrating human unity, Gilman invariably understated the range of human differences. To convey her egalitarian ideals, she insisted that everybody was as much a cell in the social body as every other body. Sometimes she denied that any differences existed at all. Although she understood that human cultures were diverse, she intended to devise a system of universalistic moral guidelines that would foster unity and discourage conflict.

As part of her overstatement of the extent of social unity in a pluralistic society, Gilman suggested that all people had identical interests and an equivalent relationship to society as a whole. In 1899, before she married, Marie Jenney, then pastoring a church in Iowa, wrote Gilman a letter about the importance of taking seriously both historical differences and ethical principles. "I have come to believe," she wrote, "that in time men and women will practice the same virtues. In the interim I could wish that men and women might attend separate churches. In the men's church I would have preached the virtues of self-sacrifice and gentleness, while the women, in their separate church, should be exhorted to self-reliance and self development."[10] Although Jenney explained her position clearly, Gilman failed to see that there was no contradiction between special group moralities on the one hand and universalistic human values on the other. Impatient with historical particularities, she persisted in arguing that everyone alike should behave according to the same splendid laws of evolutionary growth.

Gilman discussed no intermediate groupings between cell and organism-as-a-whole. Her theory of society recognized no subcommunities with shared interests and goals. White middle-class women like herself were being inhibited by conventional architecture in particular ways. They had legitimate interests in common; they shared several just grievances. Such women could reasonably combine to achieve certain goals as a step toward the achievement of a unified society of equals.

As philospher, Gilman was embarrassed by such specifics. She did not want to call attention to subdivisions in the body politic. She liked to stick to inclusive generalities. She could not bear to think about women as an interest group, much less as several rival interest groups. She hoped, by intellectual means, to do away with petty discriminations among people, binding everyone thereby into one grand human family. Ironically, her resolve to state only ethical principles that would appropriately guide everyone's behavior destined her normative system, in the final analysis, to touch no one's profoundly.

GLORY TO GROWTH IN THE HIGHEST

The second major consciousness shift on Gilman's agenda involved trading the old-fashioned world view organized around notions of conflict for a more up-to-date perspective centered on notions of growth. Convinced that only a male-dominated culture would be so preoccupied with competitive struggle, she maintained that the ongoing emancipation of women would gradually establish the more progressive root metaphor of evolutionary growth as the defining principle of society. In order to help that process along, she offered extensive instruction on the superiority of "growth" to "combat" as cultural focal point and theological symbol.

Gilman taught that growth was the innermost meaning and purpose of all animate being. Not only was God "a power promoting endless growth"; the entire content of natural law, what's more, could be rendered by the notion of "Growth."[11] Life was meant to be a garden, she fervently declared, not a battlefield. And morality consisted not of something over against nature, as most philosophers portrayed it, but of cooperation *with* nature, of developing according to one's created potential. "What we are really here for," she was fond of saying, "is Growth, Improvement, Progress. . . . Life is a Growth, a Progress, a Journey, if you will."[12]

Gilman was enthusiastic about the coincidence she saw between biological and moral laws. Like Spencer and other Social Darwinists, she stressed the location of human beings in the animal kingdom. She looked at the natural world through rose-colored glasses, seeing there an innocent arena in refreshing contrast to human history. Overlooking the predatory character of species relationships, she focused exclusively on the positive social behaviors of certain species. Unmindful of plagues, pestilence, and other natural disasters, she romanticized the state of nature and naively exhorted her contemporaries to follow their instincts. Her failure to account for the malevolence of nature as well as its beauty and sociability thus destined her evolutionary ethics to be more quaintly sentimental than seriously illuminating.

Gilman believed that three instincts were acting upon the human (as well as every other animal) species: to survive, to reproduce, and to improve. She maintainted that these universl biological laws also had important moral content. Convinced that humans were uniquely able to be self-consciously intentional about the third law, she taught that world improvement was the primary human obligation.

In emphasizing the continuity of humans with other animals, Gilman contended that morality was a feature common to all the higher animals, including ants and bees. In baptizing the biological laws of self-preservation, reproduction, and evolution into her "religion of ethics," she equated natural function with moral duty. The sum of morality, as she saw it, was contained in three rules: "To Be, To Re-Be, To Be Better." The categories of morality, according to Gilman, were applicable to all the animal species, even though the range of ethical behavior was narrower in the simpler animals.[13] To look out for oneself and to grow, to select the fittest mate with whom to produce superior children, and to improve one's social environment, in her view, were both instinctive biological impulses and serious ethical obligations.

Gilman had a lively sense of being related to "the furry babies of the forest," birds, and other "beasts of prey." She saw ubiquitous instincts at work in all animals, one of which, for example, prompted them to make homes for themselves. "This motive of home-making," she wrote, "governs the nest-builder, the burrow-digger, the selecter of caves; it dominates the insect, the animal, the savage, and the modern architect."[14] In exhorting people to follow their instincts, she believed she was teaching the fundamentals of a social ethic based on biological science. As she saw it, the new morality was empirical; it was natural; it could be easily grasped; it would become popular with the masses; it would work all things together for good.

Linking her theoretical ethics so closely to evolutionary growth created several logical and psychological problems for Gilman. Although she drew enormous hope from the conviction that history was inexorably moving in a progressive direction, she could not avoid the contradictions of such an excessive developmentalism. She would suggest, on the one hand, that the world was going to become collectivized and feminist no matter what people did or how long they dragged their feet. At other times, however, she would exhort people to stop worshiping the past and to start building a progressive future, which would require education, corrected ideas, and very hard work. She vacillated continually between a view of morality as simple alignment with nature and, alternately, morality as energetic intervention in the creation of an alternative environment.

The strand of inevitabilism in Gilman's theoretical voice was intended to alert people to the critical urgency of cooperating with evolutionary growth. Its unintended effect, however, was to jeopardize the vitality of ethical motivation. It was altogether possible—and not uncommon—to listen to such rhetoric about "irresistible uplift" and conclude that the triumph of progress was perfectly assured, whether or not particular individuals and groups roused themselves on its behalf.

Gilman believed that evolutionary growth was unambiguously good. In order to sustain such a view in the face of evidence to the contrary, she had to close her eyes to human as well as natural evil. Like many preachers of the Social Gospel, she celebrated the rational, creative, positive capacities of human beings and repudiated the morose Christian doctrine of sin. She insisted that "Our Life is not a thing spoiled in the Garden of Eden, but a long upward progress, in which the beauty and the glory far outweigh the shame."[15]

Gilman attacked the "horrid," unfair idea of orginal sin as "the heaviest weight, the darkest cloud, that ever rested on humanity." In place of the excessively negative notion of sin, she wanted to put scientific measurements of past actions as either right or wrong according to their contribution (or lack thereof) to progressive growth. In a characteristic proclamation, she declared

> This new world blazes with hope.
> We have not Sinned.
> We are not Damned.
> We do not need to be Saved.
> Our business is To Learn and To Grow.[16]

She was convinced that "One does not have to apologize to God for every foolishness, any more than a tree apologizes to the sun for worm-eaten apples."[17] Having decided past failings were irrelevant, Gilman chose to concentrate exclusively on future possibilities, with the result that most recognizable moral experience dropped from her purview.

The closest thing to human wrong that Gilman attacked was false ideas, such as "individualism" and "combat." Because she saw religion's "most pressing job" as "to clear the mind of rubbish," it followed that she would interpret Jesus not as savior but as teacher. She referred to him as "the Greatest Sociologist" and the "world-lifting sociologist" but never as redeemer or suffering servant. To explain the sorry state of the world, she looked not to "a supposititious devil" but to "our own needless stupidity," our failure to think any better than "Morons. Half-wits and quarter-wits."[18] Her portrait of immorality as practically nonexistent was the anemic underside of her rousingly enthusiastic rendering of growth both as primary metaphysical Reality and as most important ethical obligation.

As moral theorist, Gilman was so infatuated with the imperatives of progress that she saw her role as attacking not injustice, exploitation, or greed but rather all constraints on the unfolding of evolution. Her vocation was so to liquidate foolish obstacles to progress as to let "these healthful processes of change . . . have free way."[19] So unspeakably glorious was the prospect of the evolving future that no efforts were too great to hasten its realization.

By embracing evolutionary growth as the touchstone of social life, Gilman obscured many important dimensions of morality. Since there are unique aspects to the ethical experience of humans, her emphatic equation of humans with other animals precluded the possibility of intelligible ethical discussion. Her obsession with progress left no room for the subtleties of such everyday human obligations as telling the truth, for example, or keeping promises. Her apotheosis of human goodness prevented the development of her insights about justice to women. Convinced that there would always be a plentitude (and never a scarcity) of the good things of life, she did not concern herself with how the benefits of growth could be distributed fairly. Her denial of human wickedness blinded her to the importance of civil rights and the urgency of duties of noninjury. Her preoccupation with three biological laws in ascending importance as the sum of morality had no way to accommodate the universal human experiences of moral ambiguity, conflict, and quandary.

Gilman was mistaken about the unadulterated goodness of evolutionary growth. Like Bellamy, she went overboard with hopefulness in response to the increasing size, centralization, and specialization that was occurring both in industry and in the state. Her platitudes about the glories of growth could all too easily be seized as rationalizations for greed, both individual and corporate. Her moral theory thus unwittingly became a ligitimating mechanism for the imperialistic tendencies of monopoly capitalism; in effect, she was cheering for its majesty, scorning those who would constrain it, and generally distracting the attention of many would-be critics. Without any evil in the universe, there is little point in considering the nuances of social responsibility and no grounds for opposing social injustice. If there is no sin, as Gilman the philosopher maintained, then no one should have a grievance and no one is at fault.

WOMEN AS AGENTS OF SOCIAL SALVATION

Gilman looked to women to be exemplars of heroic world improvement. Although vividly aware of the injustice women suffered under patriarchal conditions, she found it uncomfortable philosophically to ask for special remedies to help repair women's injuries. Respect for gender equality, to which she was passionately committed, seemed strictly to enjoin any compensatory measures; she believed that differential treatment would suggest that women were inferior. Although disenfranchised, unequally educated, and discriminated against on every hand, women, Gilman believed, were intrinsically more than equal to men. And she summoned women as "Social Mothers" to lead the way to utopia, assuming more than half the responsibility for evolutionary growth.

Since Gilman actually saw a lot wrong with the world besides false concepts, and since she had no place for evil in her ethical theory, she often placed the blame for residual "absurdities" in the world squarely on the shoulders of women. "This is the woman's century," she wrote in the 1920s, "the first chance for the mother of the world to rise to her full place, her transcendent power to remake humanity, to rebuild the suffering world—and the world waits while she powders her nose."[20] Women could be using their newly won freedoms, she mused, to mother the world, and instead they are spending themselves foolishly in self-preoccupation and sexual adventurism.

A very complex understanding of sex differences informed Gilman's conception of heroic social motherhood. She was right in the middle of a profound cultural shift that was taking place in the popular understanding of human nature. Whereas earlier notions of maleness and femaleness suggested that gender temperaments were entirely determined by biology, it was becoming common by the turn of the century to see ways in which differing environmental conditions structured the personalities of young males and young females. Though still adhering to decidedly deterministic ideas, Gilman was an early proponent of the view that factors of social conditioning played an important role in the formation of personality structure.

The work of two greatly revered intellectuals, Sir Patrick Geddes and Lester Ward, shaped Gilman's perspective on women in important ways. The definitive theory about the nature and source of sex differences in the late nineteenth century was that of Geddes, a Scottish biologist whose experiments and theory had won him a distinguished international following. His book, *The Evolution of Sex* (1889), written in collaboration with one of his students, was widely read and discussed on both sides of the Atlantic. Among his well-known American devotees and popularizers were William James and Jane Addams, both of whose social theories clearly illustrate the extent of his influence.

Geddes observed the different behavior of spermatozoa and ova under his microscope, noting that "the males were forms of smaller size, more active habit, higher temperature, shorter life . . . and that the females were the larger, more passive, vegetative, and conservative forms."[21] Whereas the microscopic female cells tended to be more quiet and thereby to conserve energy, the even tinier male cells invariably rushed around dissipating energy. He was convinced that "man thinks more, women feels [*sic*] more. He discovers more, but remembers less; she is more receptive, and less forgetful."[22]

Geddes saw profound implications for social roles in the cellular activity he meticulously observed; he believed that it showed the social world of humans in normative microcosm. Like other scientists of the day, he did not hesitate to move freely between the descriptive realms of empirical science and the prescriptive discourse of moral philosophy.

Geddes taught that male and female energy were so radically distinct as to produce decidedly different expression in the lives of men and women. He was convinced that the conservative, constructive, more passive character of ovular activity (which he called its "anabolic tendency") proved that women were programmed by nature to develop characters that were quiet, receptive, and given to building up others. He deduced that women were endowed with a disproportionate share of the altruistic emotions and that it was therefore natural and right for them characteristically to be nurturant and self-forgetful.

Geddes's theory went on to maintain that the abrasive, destructive behavior of spermatozoa (which he called their "katabolic tendency") showed that men were destined to be the experimenters, the go-getters, the freedom-loving individualists of the species. He deduced that the egoism of males, expressed in vigorous, innovative activity, was ordained by nature as a necessary part of evolution itself.

Conveniently for the status quo, Geddes's biology of sex differences, along with its derived gender morality, coincided neatly with the dominant ideology of separate spheres. Its scientific authority was so great as to make the ideological doctrine of female altruism effectively unassailable. He preached reverence for the natural laws operative in the metabolism of ova and sperm and for the distinctive gender roles determined thereby. "What was decided among the prehistoric Protozoa," he chided, "can not be annulled by act of parliament."[23]

Like the majority of progressive intellectuals, Gilman so esteemed Geddes's work that she could not argue with his rendition of sex differences. When pressed by Professor Ross about the sources she had used in writing *Women and Economics,* she somewhat sheepishly replied that "there were only two! One was Geddes's and Thompson's [*sic*] *Evolution of Sex,* the other only an article, Lester F. Ward's, in the 1888 *Forum.*"[24]

At the turn of the century, there was no existing scientific community to challenge Geddes. Endocrinology had not yet coalesced into a coherent field of study; knowledge of the influence of sex hormones was negligible and scattered. The prevailing understanding of the biology of human inheritance was distinctly premodern; the notion of "use inheritance," the genetic transmission of acquired characteristics from one generation to another, was a standard scholarly assumption. Many traits later recognized to be profoundly affected by environmental factors were widely assumed to be simple products of heredity. In Gilman's day, among her circles of associates, there was little ground from which to doubt the validity of Geddes's findings for social theory.

The "gynaecocentric theory" of Lester Ward had a pronounced impact upon Gilman's thinking as well. She described it as "a scientific theory of more importance to the world than any put forth since the theory of evolution, and of more importance to women than any ever produced."[25]

After training as a botanist, Ward's scholarly interests moved him into the infant discipline of sociology where he established himself as an innovator in applied social science. His idealistic commitment to influencing public policy led him to spend most of his professional life in government service in Washington, D.C. The guild of sociologists named him the first president of the American Sociological Society. Toward the end of his career he was appointed to a distinguished professorship at Brown University.

Ward studied the ascending evolutionary ladder in the animal kingdom and decided that the human species had gotten off the upward track by forgetting that the female was the necessary, the first-evolved, the superior sex. He reached this conclusion after noting that the lowest, asexual species were, for all practical purposes, "maternal" in structure and that "below the vertebrates female superiority is well-nigh universal."[26] The female, in his view, predated the male in the grand evolutionary drama. She was much more nearly self-sufficient, much more highly evolved, much more crucial to evolution, unquestionably the more important partner in the reproductive processes.

Ward called his theory "gynaecocentric" to signal both the priority he associated with the female and the dissatisfaction he felt with the "androcentrism" or male-centeredness of the dominant culture. He hoped that his theory would correct an ancient falsehood and thereby make amends for the terrible injustice society had perpetrated against women. He insisted that female primacy was the correct theoretical framework in which to generate biological and sociological research. He believed that scholars of comparative culture, such as Johann Jakob Bachofen and Lewis Henry Morgan, had prepared the way for his even more startling theory with their widely read accounts of "primitive matriarchy."

It is not hard to appreciate the appeal to Gilman of Ward's ideas about female primacy. The eminent professor's theory and his prominence within the academic community emboldened her to insist upon the equal humanity of women. His belief in the essential superiority of women went a long way toward counteracting the haunting residue of presumed female inferiority being generated by prevailing ideologies of male dominance. She made her most extensive adaptation of Ward's ideas in a book entitled *Our Androcentric Culture; or, The Man-Made World* (1909). Here she documented institutional manifestations of male arrogance in such areas as sport, art, education, industry, and politics, cataloging their injuries to women, men, and society as a whole.

Relishing, repeating, and expanding Ward's arguments, Gilman took delight in the symbolic reversal implicit within the gynaecocentric perspective. It overturned the logic of the biblical creation story depicting Eve as Adam's rib. It suggested that in all actuality Adam was the evolutionary Johnny-come-lately, the derived rib from Eve's side, rather than the primal human being. The theory's mythological possibilities were considerable.

Despite the authority both Geddes and gynaecocentrism had with Gilman, she devoted an impressive amount of energy to proving that no one really knew what women are like intrinsically because the dominant culture had so powerfully trained them to be domestic servants. She maintained that no one *would* know what women are really like until women and men lived and worked in identical environments.

Gilman conducted a painstaking analysis of the moral environment produced by the ideology of gender spheres. Uncovering elements of popular wisdom that flattered woman on the one hand and insulted her on the other, she pointed out the inconsistency of putting woman on a pedestal while prating about her constitutional weaknesses. To show this, she lined up contradictory items of belief from the insulting and from the pseudo-flattering strands of ideology. How could it possibly be true, she asked, both that "women are better than men" and "women are worse than men," that they are "strong as steel" and "weak as water," childishly

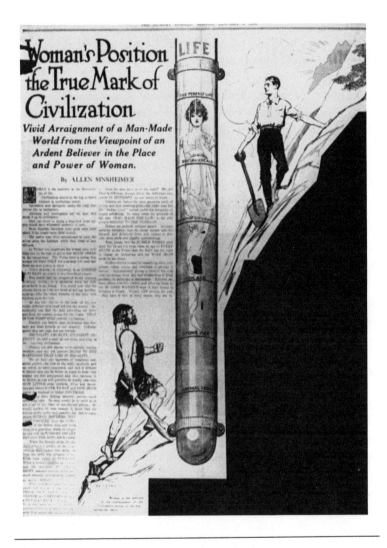

Illustration from an article discussing Gilman's woman-centered worldview in the *Boston Sunday Herald,* January 9, 1916. The drawing shows the ongoing liberation of woman as the definitive measurement of a society's progress.

"selfish" while angelically "unselfish"?[27] Though she was vigilant in objecting to insults against women's nature, it was a lot harder to resist the lures of the more flattering kind of sexist ideology. Honestly believing that science had proven woman to be superior to men, how could she seriously object to the sentimental elevation of woman to moral paragon?

Dominant gender ideology in Gilman's day insulted women as physical, intellectual, and moral beings. As an aspiring sociologist, Gilman came to women's defense on many fronts, exposing belittlement as an unfair abuse, enlisting women to join her campaign by developing strong selves. She urged women to overturn masculine morality, to observe human and not feminine standards, to be critically impatient with ideology, proudly independent, self-protectively rebellious.

Popular culture insisted that women were radically different from men, physiologically speaking; that whereas the "normal" condition of the male was hardy physical strength, the "normal" condition of the female was delicate physical vulnerability. Dependent social roles of women were said to have developed inevitably out of the given of woman's frailty, the necessities of her relatively feeble frame.

Likewise, an authoritative consensus held that a woman was uniquely determined by her sexuality, that outside of reproduction she had no significant social role. Physicians and other moralists agreed that woman's sexuality contained an implicit moral code requiring selflessness and resignation. William P. Dewees, M.D., for example, articulated a common nineteenth-century presupposition when he reported that the uterus exercised "paramount power" over woman's physical and moral systems.[28] According to conventional wisdom, women were virtual prisoners of their reproductive systems and destined thereby to be perpetual midwives to the births and rebirths of selves other than their own.

Both Gilman's life and her teaching gave the lie to the ideology concerning woman's physical weakness. When Gilman rose to speak in public, frequently wearing a self-made, well-loved plum-colored satin dress, she inspired her audiences with her robust good health, her fit, agile form, and her commitment to simplicity and comfort of dress. She celebrated physical strength and athletic accomplishment in women. She taught women "Five little rules of health": "Good air and plenty of it, good exercise and plenty of it, good food and plenty of it, good sleep and plenty of it, good clothing and as little as possible."[29]

In direct opposition to the most accepted canons concerning female beauty, Gilman urged women to choose clothing that would permit them to grow and to move, that would not exaggerate their femininity or weakness, their radical otherness. She objected in particular to "three articles, the corset, the skirt, and the shoe." She believed that the corset was "as idiotic as a snug rubber band around a pair of shears," that the skirt was a "manacle" owing to its "stricture around the waist muscles," its heavy weight, and its "friction and pressure on the legs," making it a "constant impediment." She urged women to wear only shoes in which they could stand, walk, run, and jump. She called for the abolition of high-heeled shoes, which "succeed in changing a dignified, strong, erect, steady, swift, capable, enduring instrument—the human body—into a pitiful, weak, bending, unstable, slow, inefficient, easily exhausted thing, a travesty on the high efficiency for which we are built."[30] Gilman helped create a new standard of female beauty, suggesting that only an organism that used all its faculties was truly beautiful.

Gilman frequently locked horns with those suggesting that women were completely determined by their sexuality. She warned women against neglecting their duties of "self-preservation," insisting that inattention to the development of their individual selfhood would leave each of them "a mere egg-sac, an organism with no powers of self-preservation, only those of race-preservation."[31] She urged women to deemphasize their sexuality, concentrating instead on their human qualities, their "erect posture, for instance," their "intellect . . . , instinct of workmanship . . . , [and] interest in scientific truth and the pursuit of knowledge."[32]

Gilman conducted a lifetime campaign against the ideology of female mental inferiority. Her goals were to establish that women were the intellectual equals of men and to encourage women to trust—and to extend—their rational powers. Her strategy was to show that the empirical underdevelopment of women's minds was the product of an unfair, "artificial environment" and not evidence of a lack of intellectual power. She encouraged women to be energetic with their intelligence: "Exercise your minds," she exhorted. "Look abroad. Look at the world as a whole, the people as a whole. Look up and down the ages. Review the past. Foresee the future. Stretch your brains."[33] She recalled with satisfaction that Jesus of Nazareth had saluted "the devotion . . . of Mary to the truth" and not that "of Martha to the housekeeping."[34]

As a means of reconciling her deterministic views of sexual identity with her environmentalism, Gilman developed a graphic diagram, consisting of two cut-out cardboard circles, which she used to illustrate her lectures. One circle symbolized a woman, the other a man. She darkened a

CHARLOTTE PERKINS GILMAN

LECTURER AND AUTHOR

LIST OF LECTURES

Mother, Home and Child.
⎧ Woman and Work. ⎫
⎨ Woman and Home. ⎬ Series
⎩ Woman and Child. ⎭
Public Ethics.
What Work Is.

The Real Things.
Our Brains & What Ails Them.
America's Place To-day.
End of "The Servant Question."
Body and Soul.
The Social Organism.

Generic publicity flyer from the early twentieth century advertising some of Gilman's most popular lecture topics.

narrow crescent at the outer edge of each circle to represent "the sex qualities" or distinguishing marks she associated with maleness and femaleness, respectively. She left most of the two circles empty to demonstrate the preponderance of human qualities that the male and the female possessed in common.[35]

Despite her reflective insistence that the human qualities of man and woman were far more important than their sexual ones, in less deliberative moments a lot of mischief could enter through those slender imaginary crescents of presumed sexual characteristics. What were the masculine qualities appearing on the border of the male circle? There one saw "Desire, Combat, and Self-Expression." The rest of a man's personality was said completely to overlap with a woman's . Those qualities appearing on the borders of the female circle were derived from woman's part in reproduction—"love, care, service, an active altruism"—the widely idealized "qualities of motherhood," which Gilman cited for scientific as much as sentimental reasons.

Aside from this special affinity for servanthood (which she tried to relegate to a tiny slice of the female constitution), women were constructed according to exactly the same plan that men were; there was one human blueprint with an identical set of inclinations and creative potential in both the male and the female models. Gilman occasionally reminded her readers that women actually *were* the race type, the definitive human. She did not much like to gloat about her gender's primacy, but noting it added urgency to her campaign for women's full development as human beings.

As most women know, a presumed affinity for servanthood can get out of hand—and usually does. Even though Gilman intended in her most careful moments to speak of a small portion of male and female personalities in referring to sex qualities, her ideas about gender traits had a way of expanding outward, balloon-fashion, in the general climate of the "cult of true womanhood." They overstepped themselves and seemed to describe men and women in general, not just minor tendencies within the male and female temperament.

Although capable of a judicious environmentalist constraint, Gilman, in her theoretical work, more often than not developed a doctrine of nurturant womanhood that was very oppressive to women. "The male is physiologically an individualist," she wrote, whereas the female is a socialist.[36] She sometimes baptized the straight Geddes formula into her thinking, as when she wrote that "Male energy tends to express itself in the fight, the struggle, the effort to overcome. Female energy tends to express itself in work, in growth, in the effort to serve."[37] Thus she would characterize the male personality as predominantly competitive and destructive and the female as cooperative and constructive. The conviction that female energy flowed toward making, saving, and giving whereas male energy flowed toward spending, scattering, and taking led not to a universalistic sense of responsibility for the promotion of progress but to an ethic of women doing all the work of reconciliation and justice.

THEORETICAL GRIDLOCK

Gilman became gridlocked in the toils of her synthesizing effort. To be an effective spokesperson for organic unity, evolutionary growth, and heroic womanhood, she chose to spend years and years of her life at the typewriter. She there produced an undialectical theory that was rigidly static and badly inhibiting to her feminist message. Since its doctrines involved a radical either/or-ness, she portrayed life, bewilderingly, as either social or individual, either growing or fighting, never a recognizable, comprehensible mixture. Since she had trouble allowing for moral ambiguity, she frequently overstated her case to the point of absurdity.

In her most lucid moments (usually not when she was composing ethical theory), Gilman was perfectly capable of tempering her intellectual fanaticism. In much of her poetry and fiction as well as in her sociology of the home, she stated unequivocally the ethical urgency of individual development by women. Her dialectical social psychology of sex differences, which challenged biological determinism with a robust environmentalism, represents Gilman's theory at its most cogent. Although her architectural program was a very profound means of redressing society's wrongs against women, she was inhibited theoretically from consistently representing it as such.

The notion that there is no evil in the world was Gilman's worst intellectual turn. Out of her total enchantment with evolutionary growth, she suggested that the end of progress justified any available means. She lashed out at constraints on "growth" because she had found so many circumstances in her own life constraining. But as a self-appointed spokesperson for the American social body, she implied that its leaders have a natural right to define "progress" for the masses and then to adopt policies, even coercive ones, to put that definition into effect. Without democratic constraints, that is tyranny.

Gilman had a partial appreciation of the distribution of power in the world. She knew that women as a whole had less than men as a whole. But she was blind to the variables of class and race. There is no appreciation in her theoretical work that one can be both a victim and an oppressor. She was in gridlock because she could not hold together her power and her weakness, her privilege and her injury, her love and her outrage.

The other major inhibitor in Gilman's ethics was its divorce between theory and practice. She overdosed on ideas-in-themselves. She aspired to changing people's false ideas to true ones, in part so that they would then proceed to build socialized neighborhoods. She volunteered to be a female Socrates, hoping that someday all her books, handsomely bound in a series, would fill a library shelf. Although she knew that environments determine behavior in important ways, she did not actively try to build alternative spaces herself. Because there was no way out of her theoretical system, she turned to the telling of stories to find enough room for herself.

· *CHAPTER SEVEN* ·

The Power of Gilman's Storytelling Voice

Long have we lived apart,
Women alone;
Each with an empty heart,
Women alone;
Now we begin to see
How to live safe and free,
No more on earth shall be
Women alone.

"We Stand as One"
CHARLOTTE PERKINS GILMAN

Charlotte Gilman did not agonize over the writing of her realistic short stories and novels as she did over her social ethics. Instead she wrote them casually, almost in sport. Even so, she was mindful of their educational potential. She recognized the capacity of strong fiction to move people, confiding to her diary in 1893, "If I can learn to write good stories it will be a powerful addition to my armory."

In spite of this awareness, Gilman consistently judged her philosophy to be of much greater social significance than her fiction. Except for "The Yellow Wallpaper," she scarcely mentioned her story writing in her autobiography except to say that she had written tales to help support herself and her family. In the *Forerunner*'s first year, she expressed the modest hope that her stories would provide "interest and amusement" to her readers.[1]

The realistic story, more than the utopian one, was Gilman's forte. In it she typically portrayed an ordinary white middle-class woman (or group of women) wrestling with common dilemmas that pit family obligations against individual ones. Convinced that such conflicts could best be resolved architecturally, she conjured up settings in some stage of feminist transformation for about one-third of her stories.

Gilman wanted her fiction to reinforce the individual aspirations of women. She hoped that the struggles of her imaginary heroines would encourage her female readers to take themselves seriously as autonomous actors on the stage of history. Through her stories, she tried to communicate the unfamiliar notion that women's efforts to achieve personal independence were full of moral significance.

Gilman could have said about all her fiction what she said of "The Yellow Wallpaper": "I wrote it to preach. If it is literature, that just happened."[2] Stating her aims in 1926, she wrote: "One girl reads this, and takes fire! Her life is changed. She becomes a power—a mover of others—I write for her."[3] Gilman planted her feminist ideas in fictional gardens, the artistic quality of which was only an incidental concern. Her guiding hope as storyteller was to cultivate the soil, to enlarge the common woman's sense of what was possible.

In an explicit way, the central point of Gilman's realistic fiction was to juxtapose woman's old morality of minding the domestic sphere with her new morality of responsible self-fullfilment in the world. She aimed to demonstrate conclusively both the superiority and the rightness of the new morality. She accomplished this by creating contrasting characters living by the two codes as well as characters struggling to move from the domestic code to the higher one. She was forthright about treating the moral dilemmas of women, using such titles as "Turned," "A Cleared Path," "Making a Change," "Mary Button's Principles," "Mrs. Powers' Duty," and "Mrs. Merrill's Duties."

In an implicit way, many of Gilman's stories testified powerfully to the liberating potential of nonsexist spatial design. By means of architectural backdrops, much of her fiction portrayed very tangible ways of solving the problems of isolated, overworked women. Being able to move into a more socialized dwelling or to join forces with other women in common spaces were opportunities she encouraged every woman to pursue.

MODELS OF FEMINIST ARCHITECTURE IN GILMAN'S TALES

Gilman created four types of feminist environment in her realistic fiction. In one, she portrayed apartment hotels or boardinghouses as the setting for progressively liberated life styles. In a second cluster of tales, she depicted groups of neighboring residences, linked to central facilities for laundry, child care, food delivery, and cleaning services. Women form alliances in a third group of stories, associations that meet in clubhouses to foster sisterly cooperation both in the conduct of domestic life and in training for employment outside the home. A fourth set of stories celebrates the existence of recuperative spaces, most often located in the country, run by women and for women.

Apartment Hotels and Boardinghouses

In "Forsythe and Forsythe," four professional people find romance and supportive simplicity in an apartment hotel in Seattle, Washington.[4] The name of the story refers to a man and woman, George and Georgiana Forsythe, who are husband and wife as well as cousins. Equal partners both at work and at home, they find respite from their joint practice of law in two adjoining (and distinctively decorated) apartments. Whereas George's flat is "undeniably bachelorish," there is "a wholesome femininity" in the decor of Georgiana's. Among the amenities available in the building are a restaurant on one of the lower floors and a child-care center on the roof.

In the story's rather thin plot, George's old friend Jim Jackson comes to visit Forsythe and Forsythe, at home. With a reputation for being "Rigidly conservative, even reactionary," Jackson is highly skeptical at the outset about such unorthodox living arrangements. But gradually two factors bring him around. First, "He grew used to the smooth convenience of the apartment very rapidly, even tacitly approved of the steady excellence of the food and service." Second, he can't resist the charms of the strongly independent, "mischievous" Clare Forsythe, who is George's sister and Jackson's former sweetheart. In the nine years since they have seen each other, Clare has established herself as a prominent "sanitary engineer" (plumber?), living in her own apartment in the same building as her brother and sister-in-law. Jackson finds the attraction of Clare much "greater than the repulsion caused by her limitless progressive views." Conveniently, Jackson's estranged wife mails him divorce papers just as the story ends, freeing the former skeptic to declare his love for Ms. Forsythe and to embrace her liberated life style wholeheartedly.

In "Her Housekeeper," an unusual domestic environment is instrumental in winning the heart of a beautiful actress.[5] Widowed after an unhappy marriage, Mrs. Leland is determined never to wed again. Committed to pursuing her promising career as well as protecting her freedom, she sees marriage as profoundly threatening to both. Above all, she wants to avoid domestic drudgery. "I hate—I'd like to write a dozen tragic plays to show how much I hate—Housekeeping!" she exclaims to Arthur Olmstead, a would-be suitor and fellow resident of a flourishing boardinghouse.

Slowly but surely, over a period of several months, Olmstead persuades Mrs. Leland that marriage to *him* would not involve any such dreary entrapments. As a matter of fact, he demonstrates that he has the means, the skill, and the temperament to relieve her forever of housewifely chores. He often entertains Mrs. Leland and her five-year-old son, Johnny, charmingly, in his apartment. One day he tells her that his real estate business (about which he had been purposefully vague) consists of running apartment hotels such as the one both he and she occupy. In fact, he owns their very residence as well as several others.

For as long as she had lived there, Mrs. Leland had reveled in the building's excellent cooked-food service, patronizing both the downstairs restaurant and the room-service delivery made possible by an automatic dumbwaiter attached to her flat. Furthermore, she had marveled at Mr. Olmstead's nurturant manner with children, as expressed toward Johnny. One day she complimented this remarkable man as follows: "Do you know you are a real comfort? . . . I never knew a man before who could—

well leave off being a man for a moment and just be a human creature." Convinced at last that she and Mr. Olmstead could make a very positive, unconventional marriage while maintaining (and even enhancing) their spatially supportive environment, Mrs. Leland marries "Her House-keeper" and proceeds to live happily ever after.

"Martha's Mother" is a story about the establishment of an exemplary residence club for single, working women in New York City.[6] In it, three characters, who are unacquainted at the story's beginning, collaborate to create a model environment for "working girls."

The first character is Mrs. MacAvelly, a free-lance do-gooder who has a way of always being in the right place at the right time.[7] The second is Miss Podder, a social worker, whose job with the "Girls' Trade Union Association" in New York City familiarizes her with the drearily inade-quate housing presently available to such workers. The third is a fifty-three-year-old widow, Mrs. Joyce, the mother of Martha Joyce, who is a trade union "girl" and one of the potential clients of the projected residence.

The story's first scene provides a look at the crowded, "ugly," and unhealthy conditions in which Martha and young women like her are presently living. Mrs. MacAvelly calls upon Martha and observes the environment's inadequacies. In the second scene, Mrs. MacAvelly visits a friend in the country. While there, she makes the acquaintance of the vigorous, skilled, and bored Mrs. Joyce who is now living with her widowed sister. In the course of their conversation, Mrs. MacAvelly learns that, as a farmer's wife, Mrs. Joyce has had years of experience taking in boarders; the recent widow tells her visitor that "The best time I ever had was one summer I ran a hotel." Mrs. MacAvelly tucks this information into her shrewd head and returns to New York City to initiate a new housing project.

In scene 3, Mrs. MacAvelly goes to see her old friend Miss Podder at the office of the Trade Union Association. After discussing the plight of working "girls" with jobs and rooms on the lower East Side, the two friends consider the possibility of starting a model residence club together. As they discuss the steps they would need to take in order to do so, MacAvelly tells Podder a little about Mrs. Joyce and her work history. Hoping that Joyce will agree to resolve their labor problems, they decide to proceed.

After setting out to find an appropriate building, the partners locate a large, well-equipped former boardinghouse for rent which far exceeds their specifications. Convinced that they can easily locate the twenty boarders and extra "mealers" needed to break even or better, they lease the building and start to renovate it. Then they approach Mrs. Joyce, who eagerly accepts their invitation to work as house director.

A few months later the residence opens with a full contingent of paid-in-advance occupants along with extra "table boarders." The meals are so excellent, the accommodations so "tasteful" and convenient, the opportunities for recreation so ample that there is soon "a waiting list of both sexes." Toward the end of the tale, Mrs. MacAvelly calls on Miss Podder, who had been one of the original club residents. Together they pronounce their venture a tremendous "success" of which they have reason to be "immensely proud."

A fourth story, "Her Memories," is an extended description of "Home Court," a very large apartment hotel complex on the upper West Side of Manhattan.[8] The block-square residential development, in fact, so dominates the story that the male narrator and his female companion do not have names.

What little plot the story offers consists of a convesation between two fifty-year-old friends who are "drifting along the Hudson in a safe, broad-built canoe." Looking up toward Riverside Drive and Grant's Tomb, the woman recounts the several phases of her life as experienced within the felicitous walls of Home Court. She likes the arrangement so much that she recommends it for everyone. Being a conventional sort, accustomed to detached dwellings with custom cooking (by Mom) and hands-on child care (by Mom), the man reacts to her accolades with considerable skepticism.

Home Court has all the markings of a Gilmanesque paradise. From roof to cellar the spaces in the twelve-story structures are enhanced by natural beauty, convenience, and unified construction to facilitate sharing. The complex has four buildings, each taking up an entire edge of the block. At the center of the block is a cloistered courtyard organized around a large fountain, "carved benches," and "cool arcades"; its restful ambience is enhanced by the luxuriant, well-pruned growth of fern, wisteria vines, and columbine. On the top of the four buildings are the "heavenly" roof developments, each comprising about 8,000 square feet, each connected to the other rooftops by means of bridges. The facilities atop Home Court consist of a gymnasium on one roof, a tennis court on another, a dining room/dancing space on a third, and a baby garden on the fourth. The entire roof area is planted with shrubs and flowers in which visiting birds

"The Home is Just a Place to Hang Things Up In." Cartoon mocking Gilman's architectural proposals, from the *San Francisco Examiner,* May 22, 1895.

like to perch. At the center of the formal roof garden is a "glittering" pool around which turn the woman's fondest memories of young childhood.

Inside the buildings themselves are even more wonders of communal, urban living. In the basements are the kitchens and storerooms, a second "gymnasium, bowling alley and swimming pools and baths," as well as the machinery for the production of steam and electricity. On the ground floors are the dining rooms as well as large lecture and activity rooms. On the second floors are "small clubrooms, reading-rooms and the like" for the use of both residents and outsiders, who can rent them. The remaining nine floors in all four buildings contain flats of all sizes. Having had his objections patiently answered and his admiration genuinely aroused, the man in the canoe vows to take a closer look at living options like Home Court.

Clustered Housing Served by Common Labor Centers

In a second group of Gilman's short stories, the liberated domestic environment consists of systems of linkages between households. In three of the stories, an enterprising heroine takes responsibility for establishing a domestic service and/or business in a particular neighborhood. The characters in a fourth such tale take up residence in homes already attached to such services.

Mary Watterson, the twenty-eight-year-old heroine of "A Cleared Path,"[9] owns and runs a small, diversified business in Los Angeles. Among the domestic services her "marvelous little shop" offers to the surrounding community are a small laundry, a sewing and mending bureau, and a sales outlet for children's ready-made clothing. Having been built up over an eight-year period, Watterson's business is a "model" both of exemplary labor relations (her employees, who are partners in a system of "profit sharing," have "charming work-rooms" in which to sew, mend, launder, or sell) and of "honesty, accuracy and efficiency." Spurred by the "phenomenal growth" in the city of Los Angeles, the business has done exceedingly well. As a result, the owner has branched out a bit, investing her surplus in a few pieces of real estate.

A feminist love story ensues, involving Ms. Watterson and Ransome Woodruff, a New Englander-turned-Montana-rancher, who is visiting his sister in southern California. After meeting Mary, Woodruff repeatedly extends the length of his sojourn in Los Angeles. His fascination with her proceeds from respect to passionate attraction and total commitment. Ms. Watterson's feelings for Woodruff are perfectly equivalent.

Throughout the story, Woodruff struggles to overcome his old-fashioned convictions about marriage. He believes that in circumstances like theirs the wife is the one who must relocate. This would mean that Watterson would have to give up her business and move to Montana. She wants none of that. After much soul searching, conversation, and consciousness raising, Woodruff sees the light and decides to sell his ranch so he can move to Los Angeles. He apologizes to Mary for having been "just a plain pig," and the story ends with the news that "in truth they were married the next day." Gilman thus made her point dramatically that a woman's work in the world is "a higher duty" than following her heart, especially when the work involves such "distinctly social" service to the world as a central housekeeping business.

The housekeeping service that gets reorganized communally in "Making a Change" is child care.[10] Like many of Gilman's female characters, Julia Gordins is frustrated to the point of impending insanity by the conflicting claims of her family's care and the expression of her life work. A gifted musician who had taught piano and violin before her marriage, Gordins is afflicted by the notion that a married woman must take personal responsibility for all the needs of her family. In particular, the round-the-clock demands of her newborn son, Albert, have exhausted her to the point of derangement. Julia's mother-in-law, Mrs. Gordins, who resides with the young family, has repeatedly offered her services as nursemaid. But Julia's sense of duty, pride, and wifely devotion will not permit her to accept them. And so she suffers, as do her sleepless husband and frustrated mother-in-law.

The combination of internecine hostility and chronic fatigue weigh so heavily on Gordins that one day she decides to end her life. As her husband leaves for work, she is feeling heavily despondent, but he fails to perceive it. After bumbling through the baby's bath, she uncharacteristically asks the senior Mrs. Gordins to mind the baby and proceeds to her room. After a short time, the older woman smells gas, quickly looks for its source, and, having found it, nimbly enters the transom window to rescue Julia.

In the aftermath of this crisis, the generation gap disappears. Mrs. Gordins comes to cherish the young woman as her very own daughter. As the trust between them grows, they devise a plan for starting a neighborhood child-care center on the roof and top floor of their building. The grandmother happily assumes the role of "baby garden" coordinator, furnishing the rooftop with sandpile, seesaws, swings, floor mattresses, and a shallow pool. The threefold purpose of this establishment is to allow Julia Gordins to resume her musical career, to employ the underutilized talents of the senior Mrs. Gordins, and to provide a much-needed social service. Gilman frequently suggested in her stories that women's intergenerational needs for self-expression, like those of the older and the younger Mrs. Gordins, should be approached simultaneously, in a complementary, mutually supportive manner.

"Old Mrs. Crosley" is another story in which a felicity of matched needs is found.[11] Here Gilman expressed concern for the middle-aged woman facing the "empty nest" syndrome. Written when Gilman herself was fifty-one, it is a morality tale about a fifty-two-year-old woman who decides there can be meaningful life after her last baby marries and becomes a father.

In the first part of the story, Mrs. Crosley is depressed because of her age and her lost raison d'être. Her three children are living their own lives in three distinct cities. Mr. Crosley, her fifty-four-year-old husband, has entered a new phase of his life by taking up politics, which he loves. Mrs. Crosley feels apathetic, unskilled, and lonely. Although her home runs smoothly and comfortably, she does not take pride in that fact because she believes she owes it all to her two servants, a cook and a maid.

One evening when she is feeling particularly old and worthless, Mrs. Crosley receives a visit from John Fairmount, the young minister of her church. Expressing his sympathetic concern for her as a fellow human soul, the Reverend Mr. Fairmount assists Mrs. Crosley in identifying an important skill she possesses but has never acknowledged. She is a great personnel manager. She has had extraordinary success in hiring household workers, training them, and maintaining their morale. She is the only woman in town with "excellent servants." He urges her to turn this unusual ability into a community venture.

Over the objections of her husband and children, Mrs. Crosley starts a business that trains and furnishes household help on either an hourly or a permanent, full-time basis. Her "Newcome Agency" offers centralized services as well as a labor bureau. She puts some of her well-trained laborers to work running a laundry and a cooked-food shop. In addition to getting her started, John Fairmount continues to give her support and encouragement, drumming up business for her agency wherever he goes.

The female characters in "The Cottagette" are patrons rather than proprietors of central housekeeping facilities.[12] Malda, who narrates the story, and her close friend Lois decide to take up residence in a cottage at

"High Court" for a summer. Malda is a needlework artist who draws subjects from nature before transcribing them onto fabric. Lois is a pianist. They are attracted to High Court both by its natural setting and by its liberty from household chores. Set high on a wooded mountainside, their dwelling comes with one big and two little rooms and, luxuriously, "a real bathroom." It has no kitchen because it was built to be serviced by "a central boarding house nearby" where residents take their meals, less than two minutes' walk from their front door. The two women flourish with so much free time for the practice of their art, surrounded by "the green shadiness, the soft brownness, the bird-inhabited quiet flower-starred woods."

Such a place proves to be an auspicious setting for romance as well. Ford Mathews, a writer and fellow resident of High Court, develops a friendship with both women and a particular affection for Malda. In the main action of the story, Lois, who is the older (and presumably wiser) of the two women, persuades Malda that the best (and perhaps the only) way to win the hand of Mathews in marriage is to add a kitchen to their residence. Convinced that a house must have a kitchen to qualify as a real "home," the women arrange to have the High Court management install a simple kitchen in their cottage.

During the ensuing months, Malda devotes herself to fixing "delicious little suppers" for Mathews and other guests, waiting for deliveries of meat, milk, and produce, baking bread, and always feeling "the call of the kitchen" as soon as she wakes. As a result she has almost no time for her drawing and embroidering. But she rationalizes her choice along the following bittersweet lines: "What was one summer of interrupted work, of noise and dirt and smell and constant meditation on what to eat next, compared to a lifetime of love?" Furthermore, she is resigned to the view that marriage and kitchen tending go hand in hand so she "might as well get used to it."

One fine afternoon toward the end of the summer, Mathews invites Malda to go on a hike for which he has prepared a "perfect lunch." On their way down the mountain, Mathews asks Malda to be his wife, but on one remarkable condition. "You mustn't cook!" he says. "You must give it up—for my sake." Instead of basking in her culinary attentions, this paragon of maleness has been suffering all summer "to see my woodflower in a kitchen." He declares to Malda: "Your work is quite too good to lose; it is a beautiful and distinctive art, and I don't want you to let it go." Then he withdraws the condition if she insists that she really *must* cook. (She is incredulous.) To his tender inquiry as to whether she can possibly give up domesticity, Malda ends the story with the following exclamation: "Could I? Could I? Was there ever a man like this?"

Women's Clubhouses for Domestic and Nondomestic Cooperation

Gilman told several stories about what women could do collectively to augment their individual powers. Pending the development of domestically integrated neighborhoods, she advocated the establishment of women's alliances everywhere so that women could meet together regularly for recreation and collaboration. Since there were not many socialized residential areas with shared services at the time she wrote, these tales were aimed to show readers how they might get such facilities started.

Gilman set two of these stories in England: "A Council of War" and "A Surplus Woman."[13] Though neither has as much dramatic vitality as the best of her stories, these two British tales set forth in succinct fashion Gilman's sense of feminist political strategy.

Although "A Council of War" is very diffuse, this earlier story contains some tough realism about the bitter conflicts aroused by women's struggle for empowerment. In it a group of "between twenty and thirty" women meet in London for a conversation about their frustrations and their strategic options for overcoming them. They discuss sexism, antifeminist backlash, their abstract sense of idealistic purpose, and their concrete goals for "the enlargement of women." Considering the possibility of a long-term strike to achieve higher wages, the vote, and gender equality throughout society, these trade unionists and suffragists brainstorm about political tactics.

The wide-ranging "war" that results exemplifies Gilman's penchant for global analysis and her weakness as a practical tactician. Within a few minutes of conversation, the women decide to establish a "great spreading league of interconnected businesses" owned and faithfully patronized by women. They also resolve to acquire halls in which to speak, and paper mills, printing shops and publishing offices, which will help spread their message of liberation. Accepting no limits on their entrepreneurial ambitions, they agree in addition to start "a perfect chain of Summer boarding houses," a laundry business, and an employment agency connected to a "Training School for Modern Employment." A committee of three, appointed at the close of the story, is instructed to consult "widely" on these

Cartoon by Gilman juxtaposing a photograph of Houghton Gilman's face inside a friendly caricature.

far-reaching schemes and to report back at the next meeting. The story ends on an expectant note: "and the women looked at one another with the light of a new hope in their eyes."

"A Surplus Woman," though similar in format, shows how Gilman refined the enthusiasms expressed in the earlier story. The emerging organization here is less militantly confrontational and considerably more focused.

Susan Page, a young British woman whose father, brother, and lover have all been killed in the World War, bravely faces the social implications of the war's liquidation of a "whole generation of masculine youth." Determined that women make the best of their necessary singleness, she envisions new opportunities for female bonding which would not exist if young women like herself were all starting families.

Page calls a meeting of five women to propose that they form a "Women's Economic Alliance" with branches throughout England. The WEA's underlying purpose would be to enable single women to become productive members of society. Her plan calls for a strong emphasis on training, with "employment agencies" in every locale. Each local branch would conduct an "economic census" of women and then proceed to establish appropriate classes and eventually a "high grade vocational college" with traveling lecturers and libraries.

After persuading them to join her and then actually training large numbers of women, Page and her new colleagues organize domestic service businesses, run by the newly trained women, all over the country. Like the women in the first story, these look forward in the long run to the establishment of residential clubhouses with shared facilities. But in this second tale of British sisterhood, Gilman showed a more mature sense of what was possible, a more restrained sense of agenda, a greater realism. Its increased sense of political strategy makes for a better story, too.

The establishment of clubhouses for the congregating of women is accomplished by individual women in two other *Forerunner* stories. In "Mrs. Hines' Money," a recently widowed forty-eight-year-old woman determines to put her inherited wealth "to work for righteousness."[14] Having been subtly oppressed in her marriage and severely injured in the accident that killed her husband, Mrs. Hines spends two years in rest, exercise, travel, and study. She believes that the securing of "vigorous health" for herself is the necessary first step in "doing the most good" she can with her money and real estate.

When she returns to her rather provincial hometown, she is so invigorated as to feel that she has "changed from a mouse to an elephant." Her study and travel have helped her clarify what she wants to do. On a "conveniently situated lot," which was in her inherited portfolio, she erects a building to serve and bring the community together. It is equipped with athletic facilities in the basement, an activity center on the roof, an auditorium, a circulating library, large and small clubrooms, and an "airy restaurant." To her surprise and pleasure, the Hines Building turns out to be a profitable venture, earning income 10 percent above its expenses and promising to replenish her capital in ten years' time.

In "Three Thanksgivings," another widow, Delia Morrison, establishes a built environment for the communal edification of women.[15] Without the liquid assets of Mrs. Hines, Morrison executes her plan over the strenuous objections of both her two children and her suitor and creditor, Peter Butts.

Mr. Butts owns the mortgage on Ms. Morrison's spacious home. Since it is coming due in two years' time and since he is interested in marrying her, the banker presses his suit in largely economic terms. He is confident she has no other way to pay him off. Both Morrison's married children, regarding her as helpless and over the hill, beg their mother to come live with them. Delia Morrison is not interested. She wishes to stay in her beloved home, inherited from her father, to do something constructive for the community, and to find a way to support herself.

After making a thorough inventory of her household and its furnishings, Morrison decides to take a bold step. With the help of her black servant, Sally, she turns her home into the headquarters for the "Haddleton Rest and Improvement Club." Here, the (presumably white) middle-class women's community gathers regularly, for domestic collaboration, educational programs, and recreation.

After one year, thanks to a carefully managed membership system to which 500 women belong, Morrison has not only paid off her mortgage but cleared $1,000 in profit. Securely rid of Mr. Butts, Morrision's project becomes more and more successful in succeeding years. Gilman here testified to the importance of economic independence to women, offering practical lessons on one middle-class way to achieve it.

Women's Recuperative Spaces

In another group of stories, Gilman featured special places where women (and sometimes men) could go for rest, recreation, and healing. A number of summer resorts like the ones portrayed here were actually built, incorporating Gilman's specifications for connected, kitchenless facilities. Apart from their ordinary lives, women find here both new forms of therapeutic togetherness and opportunities for refreshing solitude.

"Girls and the Land" is the story of Dacia Boone, a young woman living in Seattle, Washington.[16] Like the novel *What Diantha Did,* this story is a detailed set of directions on how to create a Gilmanesque space.

With a very shrewd business sense and a sturdy contentment with her life style as a single woman, Dacia Boone is impervious to her mother's worries about her homeliness; she turns a deaf ear to Mom's frequent exclamation, "If only you had been a man!" She sets out to accumulate enough wealth both to assist her stepfather in a development project and to build a "Vacation Place" in the country where groups of "working girls" from clubs throughout the state can go for two weeks of wholesome camping. Along with many fiscal details about how she accomplishes this, the story shows Dacia making a stunning success of both building projects. In the course of her enterprising activity, she also meets a talented carpenter/designer, Olaf Pedersen, with whom she starts a furniture business and falls in love.

"Maidstone Comfort" is a "rambling summer settlement" at the seashore.[17] It comes into existence as the result of a timely collaboration orchestrated by a "quiet, adaptable, middle-aged" character by the name of Benigna MacAvelly.

Sarah Maidstone Pellett owns a considerable amount of remote, beach-front property, which her domineering husband will not let her develop. MacAvelly introduces Pellett to Molly Bellew, a floundering twenty-year-old rebel who is on the threshold of inheriting millions of dollars. Together Pellett and Bellew build and manage a beautifully restorative seaside compound which is also handsomely lucrative.

Maidstone Comfort, like Gilman's utopian places, combines natural beauty with architectural integration. A whole village of small, brightly colored cottages is built along curving streets beside the shoreline; luxuriant flowers, vines, and shrubs adorn the areas between them. Convenient to all of the houses is a hotel at which guests can take excellent meals. As an additional service, "a brisk motor-wagon" equipped with "neat receptacles" is primed, upon receipt of a phone call, to deliver outstanding food to a cottage's back door and to return later to pick up the dirty dishes. No one who comes to this place for recuperation has to give a single thought to the question of what to eat.

"The Jumping-Off Place" is a popular boarding hotel located in the country near a place identified only as Crosswater.[18] This amusing story is an extended polemic demonstrating both the splendid satisfaction to single women of economic independence and the decadent emptiness of certain other life styles. That the heroine's work is managing a resort famous for the quality of its service was somewhat incidental to Gilman's didactic purpose here. Nonetheless, the story conveys the message that spaces like the Jumping-Off Place fulfill a function crucial to social progress.

Fifty-seven-year-old Jean Shortridge is the founder/proprietor of this country hotel. Since she has never married or had children, two prospective guests feel very sorry for her. Indeed, at age forty-eight, Shortridge had experienced a number of reversals that had almost stymied her. But being a resilient, resourceful sort, she had refused to be defeated. Scoffing at those who say life is over by the age of fifty, she proved that one can actually start a new life at fifty. Now she grows fruits and vegetables worthy of a champion horticulturalist, preserves and cans the excess for commerical sale, and competently directs all the operations of her model rest accommodations.

To underline the moral of the story, Jean Shortridge declines an offer of marriage in the last scene. Her suitor is one of the formerly patronizing guests who is now beside himself with admiration. He is a handsome clergyman toward whom Shortridge had once felt worshipful adoration. The heroine has independent plans for the remainder of her life, having learned wisdom from her years of growth and hard work. After declining Dr. Whitcomb's proposal, she says to herself, "Why should I? . . . I always hated nursing." And we see that Gilman regards this Jumping-Off-Place as an opportunity for fulfillment superior to conventional marriage.

Although "Dr. Clair's Place" is a "psycho-sanatorium" known as "The Hills," it resembles Gilman's resort places in many particulars.[19] Built on the southern face of the Sierra Madre, it specializes in the cure of neurasthenia or melancholia in women. Besides extensive facilities for the holistic cure of the sick, The Hills also includes simple small and large cottages and tent-houses where well persons can stay. Dr. Clair invites the relatives and friends of ailing women to come for a while to be near their loved ones. She believes that having strong, healthy people on the premises is encouraging to all of the patients. That it is a highly agreeable place is underscored by the fact that cured people keep coming back for holidays, and there is "usually a waiting list" from the population at large.

This particular story follows a "Despairing One," Octavia Welch,

Looking back on her life. Photograph of Gilman by Doris Ulmann, about 1930.

through the various stages and settings of Dr. Clair's therapy. After about a month of "bedroom and balcony treatment" in which the accent is on sleep, baths, massage, and good food, she moves to a "halfway house" which is "up the canyon." Here she spends another month of "physical enlargement," in which she swims, climbs mountains, and generally exerts herself to the point of "plain physical exhaustion." The importance of rest is emphasized in this setting as well. Upon finishing her stint at the halfway house, she takes up permanent residence in a little cottage set aside for well patrons. Like the other residents, both short- and long-term, she takes her meals at the community cafeteria. Now she earns her living by needlework and the teaching thereof, regarding herself, contentedly, as a lifelong "Associate" of The Hills.

THE IMPORTANCE OF STORIES TO GILMAN'S VISION

In short, modest stories about white middle-class and upper-middle-class women, Gilman unselfconsciously made her most compelling argument for nonsexist architecture. To dwell imaginatively for a few moments in a landscape with connected domestic facilities suggests powerfully that such environments are both desirable and achievable.

As the backdrop for dozens of Gilman stories, socialized feminist spaces need no elaborate rationale. Their vitality is compelling in and of itself, representing the way the landscape will look when empowered women learn to look out for their own interests. In contrast to the distorting one-sidedness of her philosophical universe, here individuality is reassuringly secure, celebrated in the struggles of heroines to achieve personal autonomy. In the world of Gilman's realistic fiction, growth and conflict, individuality and connectedness, uncertainty and ambiguity are all experienced and taken into account. Except for the recurrent figure of Mrs. MacAvelly, no character is portrayed mothering other people endlessly without looking after her own needs.

Gilman's realistic fiction corrected for her theoretical excesses. She located its characters squarely in the familiar flux of history where decisions and actions were always conditioned by the necessities of space and time. Here no one gives any thought to the abstract normative considerations discussed in her formal ethics; the actors show no concern for conforming themselves to evolutionary laws. Nor are they obsessed with their duty to self-efface in deference to the ideal of social unity.

In recent years the humble narrative has come into its own as a bearer of ethical meaning. Recognized in women's consciousness-raising groups as a crucial mode of empowerment, its capacity to enliven moral principles has recently been noted by both activists and academics.

A contemporary philosopher, Stanley Hauerwas, has written appreciatively about the ethical significance of stories, recognizing in them a necessary complement to normative abstractions. He reminds moral theorists of their creative dependence on descriptive narrative, lest they forget and attempt to survive in the realms of "pure" cogitation. He writes, "If our lives are to be reflective and coherent, our moral vision must be ordered around dominant metaphors or stories." He discusses the everyday process by which we form our character and virtue, indeed the very story of our lives, in response to stories that have captured our imagination. At his most enthusiastic, he claims: "To be moral persons is to allow stories to be told through us . . . Our experience itself, if it is to be coherent, is but an incipient story."[20] At times more aware of it than at others, Gilman's own life story as well as the rich produce of her literary imagination provided an invaluable grounding to her lifelong project of social ethics.

Gilman's realistic stories help reconstruct the heart of her vision for the built environment. More than anything else, she wanted to liberate women from solitary, burdensome housework. To that end she urged women to pursue as many strategies as they could think of appropriate to their particular location and circumstance. Where possible, they should live in socialized residences attached to commercialized domestic services. If there were none, they should consider starting one, even a very informal, small-scale service, with the hope that it would grow. They should talk to each other about what they need. They should meet in large and small groups and try to solve their problems collectively. They should form alliances.

Men are not without significant roles in Gilman's stories. Dozens of them see the light and choose to live in liberated households. A few even engage in domestic work themselves, most notably Ford Mathews in "The Cottagette," who fixes a "perfect" picnic lunch and begs his fiancée to stop doing housework, and Arthur Olmstead in "Her Housekeeper," who looks after children and develops admirable apartment hotels. Although the challenge of involving men equally in housework was not high on Gilman's agenda, a few of her stories suggest that she would appreciate the justice of such a campaign.

· CHAPTER EIGHT ·

Conclusion

In the name of your ages of anguish!
In the name of the curse and the stain!
By the strength of your sorrow I call you!
By the power of your pain!

. . . .

In the name of our ages of anguish!
In the name of the curse and the stain!
By the strength of our sorrow we conquer!
In the power of our pain!

"The Burden of Mothers"
CHARLOTTE PERKINS STETSON

The social landscape of family and productive life in the United States has continued to change in the decades since Charlotte Gilman dreamed her dreams. Two of the most striking modern phenomena affecting the environment have been the American love affair with the automobile and the building of suburbia. Instead of living in apartment hotels in compact urban settings, as Gilman envisioned, a growing proportion of middle-class families, during the twenties, thirties, forties, and fifties, moved to strictly residential tracts outside the central city, enclaves that depended very substantially on the use of a privately owned car.

For most of the twentieth century, it has been people with the least amount of social and political leverage, notably individuals and families with relatively low income, who have inhabited our central cities. As increasing numbers of young male and female professionals and well-to-do-couples, often with two hefty paychecks, have decided in the last two decades to reclaim the urban spaces abandoned by their parents and grandparents, city people on modest incomes have commonly been displaced from their neighborhoods by sky-rocketing rents, condominium conversions, and/or urban renewal. During the 1980s, the richest nation in the world has forced a hauntingly large number of its citizens into a homeless underclass for whom the idea of any kind of secure roof over their heads has become a cruelly unattainable dream.

These trends have made it even more difficult to envision (much less demand and/or build) socialized neighborhoods. Over the decades, private building projects, government housing policies, and mortgage-lending practices have taken advantage of the generous expanse of the American continent at the expense of the cooperative impulse (as well as the natural environment). Lobbyists for car manufacturers and businesses servicing automobiles as well as the avidly consuming public itself have seen to it that elected officials and city planners throughout the century have devoted a great deal more attention to the building of an elaborate network of highways than they have to developing comprehensive systems of child care, dining, and other structures of domestic support.

Over the same period, demographic trends have resulted in a population in which the nuclear-family type, for which almost all suburban (and urban) housing was built, represents a shrinking proportion of the whole. As life expectancy, especially women's, has steadily increased, planners and builders have noticed that shared domestic facilities, attached to private spaces, constitute a far superior living environment for the elderly, especially the *single* elderly. Congregate housing for senior citizens represents the most substantial development of socialized dwellings yet built in the United States, outside of such institutional settings as college dormitories, jails, armed services' barracks, hospitals, hotels, convents, and monasteries.

Other increasing constituencies for domestically serviced housing have not been as quickly recognized by the building community. One very significant group is the growing number of families in which there is no full-time homemaker. In situations where a single parent works full time and runs a household, or even when more than one adult try to juggle work and family obligations, there is a crying need, especially where income is low, for institutionalized assistance with the processes of feeding, cleaning, caring for dependent persons such as the very young and the very old, doing laundry, and the like. Households composed of one person living alone make up another expanding group for whom the optional sociability and domestic convenience of residential interdependence has a special appeal.

Instead of planned, coordinated living environments with incorporated domestic services, most middle- and working-class individuals and families today have to make do with strictly piecemeal substitutes. Most families with small children cannot find an adequate child-care facility, much less find one in a convenient location. Likewise, only a small proportion of the senior citizens who need it can now purchase one hot meal per day, delivered, from a service organization such as Meals on Wheels. To give working parents a break from cooking, a family can patronize McDonald's or order pizza once or twice a week; more prosperous households can purchase quality frozen food (if they are lucky enough to find a commercial supplier) or go to finer restaurants. Only families with considerable income can afford to employ a servant, commercial laundries, and/or cleaning establishments; most people have to either do their own cleaning when they are tired, often during precious time-off from employment, or else learn to live with chaos.

Although it has been subtle and difficult to trace, Gilman's direct influence on the built environment was most apparent in the early decades of this century. She herself was more inclined to exhort than to organize communities to build supportive neighborhoods. Impressed with Gilman's ideas, a New York group called the Feminist Alliance, founded by Heterodoxy member and school activist Henrietta Rodman, *almost* built a twelve-story building of kitchenless apartments in Greenwich Village in 1914 and 1915; a coalition of innovators and philanthropists, which had secured extensive architectural drawings and even purchased a site, broke down over ideological issues. At about the same time, Alice Constance Austin, a gifted, self-educated California architect, responded explicitly to the designs of Gilman (and Gilman's kindred architectural spirit in England, Ebenezer Howard) in her work. She developed extensive plans for kitchenless houses set in a socialist garden city. Although only a few individual houses were built to her specifications, her 1916 site plan for a city to be called Llano del Rio is still a brilliant, if unbuilt, synthesis of architectural and social innovations.[1]

Two noteworthy projects in New England, dating from the 1920s, arose in acknowledged response to Gilman's educational efforts. Yelping Hill, a cooperatively owned summer colony in West Cornwall, Connecticut, consisted of kitchenless cottages attached to common living and dining rooms, served by a child-care program; begun by an editor and an educator, with their spouses and friends, the facilities were in operation every summer until World War II. Also in the 1920s, Ethel Puffer Howes, an accomplished philosopher/psychologist with a husband and two children, "decided to devote the rest of her career to political organizing on domestic issues." With funding from the Laura Spellman Rockefeller Foundation, she established the Institute for the Coordination of Women's Interests in Northampton, Massachusetts, which Hayden describes as "the most complete campaign yet mounted" for the implementation of Gilmanesque programs. For about five years, beginning in 1927, the Institute offered Northampton residents the opportunity to purchase inexpensive cooked food (delivered) from a community kitchen, house-cleaning services, and child care. Although initially supportive, the faculty and trustees of Smith College became skeptical of the value of Howes's intensely practical concentration on "women's interests," and their repudiation eventually caused the Institute to lose its funding. Between 1924 and 1930, commercial cooked-food services as well as neighborhood dining clubs were being developed and operated in dozens of communities throughout the country.[2]

Although Gilman's influence on neighborhood design appears to have been less direct in succeeding decades, occasional residential projects (and even entire communities) were built according to her specifications. In the late 1920s, for example, the City Housing Corporation of New York City built two residential communities, the integrated design and shared facilities of which followed significant parts of Gilman's program. Both remain in use to this day. Sunnyside Gardens in Queens is comprised of brick row houses surrounding large interior courtyards and day-care facilities. Radburn, New Jersey, is a planned, white-collar community, the shared parks of which were designed to foster friendly, interhousehold cooperation.[3]

In the 1930s, Franklin Roosevelt's New Deal gave some momentum to the development of socialized communities. Under the leadership of Rexford Tugwell, the Resettlement Administration created three suburban greenbelt towns (in Maryland, Wisconsin, and Ohio) in which a concerted effort was made to integrate work and home life. The Public Works Adminstration, advised by Catherine Bauer, made federal money available to build a type of housing for workers with extensive shared recreational and service facilities. An outstanding built example can be found in the Carl Mackley Houses in Philadelphia.[4] In the 1940s, Vanport City, Oregon, and Baldwin Hill Village, California, were new towns explicitly built to give social and architectural support to family women who were gainfully employed in war-related industries.[5]

In the last forty years, unified neighborhoods have been constructed in several places around the world, giving built expression to Gilman's communal ideal. The kibbutzim in Israel are the best known example. In addition, the Swedish governement has cooperated with private developers in building a number of socialized residential facilities. With the important encouragement of Alva and Gunnar Myrdal, several "service" or "collective houses" have been built in Sweden since 1938, serving anywhere from 8 to 1,200 distinct housing units. Sometimes purchased separately and at other times included in the rent, these "houses" offer an impressive range of services, including "meals from a central kitchen; day care for children between the age of six months and seven years; activities and day rooms for other people; hobby rooms for clubs and individuals; day and night laundries; maternity and well-baby clinics; and help in arranging for baby-sitting, house-cleaning, plant-watering (during vacation) and errand-running (for the sick)."[6] More recently, serviced residential projects geared specifically to the needs of single mothers have begun appearing in both Europe and the United States, for example, the Nina West Homes in London, the Mothers' House project in Amsterdam, and the Willowbrook Demonstration project in the Watts neighborhood of Los Angeles.[7]

BEYOND GILMAN'S INTELLECTUAL AND POLITICAL GRIDLOCK

Although Gilman's fondest hope was to write a formal social ethic that was both universalistic and timeless, she occasionally indicated that she knew that the task was beyond her. In February 1914, for example, she mused about the obscurity of her subject matter. "So complex, so confused, so contradictory," she wrote, "is this field of social perception, that in order to form any clear idea of it we must study it from the side."[8] She frequently recommended cultivating the perspective of an outsider, an unbiased observer, such as a traveler from a strange, radically different place. Despite her repeated efforts to portray moral life in the abstract, she had her greatest success when she stopped trying. "It is a wonderful thing," she wrote, "to change your focus, to draw off a bit, and see life sideways."[9] Gilman fashioned a solution to the philosophical conundrums that ensnared her "from the side."

It was when she approached social ethics obliquely, in architectural analysis and fable, that Gilman made her most important feminist statement. As a utopian writer of moral theology, she was crippled by her fervent indebtedness to evolutionism, biological determinism, and social organicism. Stuck in an idealistic vise from which she could not extricate herself, her philosophical ideas were often directly at odds with her deepest convictions.

Gilman forged a congenial idiom for the expression of her ethical concerns when she was least self-conscious about them. Unencumbered by philosophical dualisms, she strongly set forth the power of a male-centered, female-despising culture both to fortify men and to undermine women. When she drew directly upon her own experience, she was able to be intellectually clear, straightforward, and powerful. Standing in the real world of hungry people and dirty laundry, she was less susceptible to distorting intellectual enthusiasms. Her compassion for her own and other women's very palpable domestic suffering infused her voice with an authority that her more pretentious efforts at philosophy never attained.

Serendipitously, the heroines of Gilman's fiction conveyed her most coherent normative messages, embodying themes far more subversive of existing gender relationships than she was able to state explicitly in her philosophy. "Don't let yourselves be trampled on," she thus entreated her women readers, subtly and unsubtly. "Go after what you need in order to be autonomous, self-supporting citizens." "Be loyal to other women."

"Organize yourselves to achieve small, realistic goals." Like many good teachers, Gilman was able to speak in parables things she was inhibited from saying directly.

Gilman understood that the best way to change people's ideas was first to revise their material circumstances, their physical environments, their patterns of interaction. The shrewdness of her architectural perspective demonstrates this. But she herself disdained the applied, organizing side of so proceeding. Exaggerating the power of ideas in themselves to set meaningful social change in motion, she contented herself with instructing the public in the superiority and rightness of environmental change. She worked indefatigably, as journalist, educator, and general cheerleader for the cultivation of progressive attitudes. But she did not develop a long-term political base from which to practice what she preached. With her magazine, books, poetry, and lectures as pulpit, she composed a lot of good sermons. But her efforts actually to implement her architectural understandings were much fewer and farther between.

Three problems in the way Gilman approached her work continue to bedevil many white feminists today, almost one hundred years later. The comfortable advantages of her economic and racial circumstances, in the first place, lulled her into a distorting, sometimes dangerous false consciousness. Owing to privileges of class and skin color, she was able to buy her way into the country's elite intelligentsia, and she chose to do so. In her view, the patriarchal institutions of capitalism were not so much evil as they were behind the times. She set out therefore not to change them but to improve them, to correct their false ideas, to integrate their ruling classes with women. Insofar as she joined the white male intellectual establishment, Gilman relinquished much of the power of her vision as an outsider. As philosopher, she lost touch with insights drawn from her own, often-bitter experience. She became in effect a scintillating spokeswoman for the hierarchical culture that oppressed her. In becoming an intellectual's intellectual, she accepted the divorce of reason from emotion that is still highly revered in some academic circles, thus rendering her formal ethical analysis, for all practical purposes, impotent.

A second problem Gilman had, which continues to persist in much of the work of contemporary white middle-class feminists, involves the question of what to do with one's legitimate anger. In the Victorian era even more than in our own, the expression of anger was deemed unfeminine, unladylike, even uncivilized. As a result, gender mores in her day probably had as much to do with Gilman's euphoric outlook as did the pervasive intellectual vogue of progressive optimism. White men, in whose hands was concentrated the lion's share of economic and political power (not to mention the physical strength), were to be persuaded and won over, not blamed and antagonized. Gilman therefore went to extreme lengths to explain sexism as a necessary stage in social progress, suggesting that the "unspeakable injustice and cruelty" that women had experienced had been "essential . . . that man might slowly rise to full racial equality with [them]."[10] Lacking anyone to blame, she turned her anger on herself, spending years of her life in a state of severe depression. Denying how bad things really were, she consistently urged herself and her comrades to emphasize the positive, to mother people, to improve the world. Because she tried to define them out of her universe, the forces of evil often caught her unawares, badly draining her strength and demoralizing her. Resistance to evil, collectively and individually, was not a recognized human obligation in Gilman's system of ethics. The omission cost her dearly, requiring that she continually deny or absorb her own anger.

The third problem in Gilman's ethical method was its denial of human differences. Having been so wounded by the designation "other" in the dominant culture, she set out to include everyone in her philosophical embrace. There were no groups in Gilman's theory of society, only individuals (cells) and the total organism (society). She had only the most rudimentary analytic handles for thinking about relationships between classes and ethnic groups. Related to her problem with anger, she preferred to believe in an abundance and not a shortage of the good things in life. She therefore could not appreciate the way in which powerful interests were cynically emphasizing differences of race, gender, ethnicity, and class in order to divide popular consciousness and thereby maintain control over the distribution of scarce resources. In her extensive vision of socialized, woman-supporting neighborhood design, she made her most cogent effort explicitly to promote the combined interests of professional and working-class people on the one hand and all women on the other. But in what Adrienne Rich would call her "snow-blindness," her thinking, imagining, and speaking "as if whiteness described the world," Gilman's "passive collusion" with institutionalized racism revealed a despicable "form of naivete and moral stupidity." The major failing of Gilman's imagination was in not noticing the social poison of racial segregation, in not joining what Rich has called our "strong antiracist female tradition," which has a history predating even the Abolitionists.[11]

Despite her pretensions on behalf of authoritative social theory, Gilman was able to retain, on the side, her grasp of the political significance of housework and its architectural setting. In her sociology of the home, her poetry, and her realistic fiction, she gave that insight its most memorable expression. In demonstrating the arbitrariness of conventional neighborhood design and the unfairness of requiring women to bear the domestic burdens of men, she made her most enduring contribution to the ongoing development of socialist-feminist understandings.

During the last twenty years of reanimated women's movements, many black and white feminists in the United States have cultivated a holistic, global perspective centered on the position of women, akin to the one Gilman was attempting one hundred years ago. Whereas Gilman, without benefit either of citizenship or of higher education, was struggling against customs forbidding women either to speak in public or to assert their own wills, recent feminists, with greater access to the insights of modern psychology, intergroup relations, and cross-cultural anthropology, have sought to understand the interlocking systems of class, race, and gender oppression. While Gilman was threatened by the acknowledgment of economic and/or ethnic difference, modern feminists have learned that an absolute commitment to liberty and justice for all is woefully incomplete without exactly such acknowledgment, that detailed awareness of the particular (relative) circumstances of different groups just as much as the unwavering ideals of ethical absolutism are necessary, complementary ingredients of a complete social morality.

There is much we can learn from Gilman's errors. She and subsequent generations of feminists have undoubtedly made our contemporary struggles for survival and dignity less fearsome. Today we know that breaking out of our present versions of intellectual and political gridlock will require us to accept and channel our personal and collective anger; we have begun to learn how to do so. Likewise, from a late twentieth-century perspective it is easier to see the urgency of integrating our analytic powers with our passion for social justice and of helping one another to harmonize our theory and our practice.

Tutored by the political experience and raised consciousness of the last three decades, many people have learned through engaged struggle and subsequent dialogue that difference does not have to entail relations of dominance and submission. Convinced that "the mere tolerance of difference between women is the grossest reformism." Audre Lorde sets forth a profoundly positive notion of such interpersonal differences as class, race, and ethnicity, advocating a politics that will "take our differences and make them strengths."[12] Likewise, Adrienne Rich poetically evokes the same possibility for a pluralistic women's movement, suggesting that only when "We drink at each other's difference . . . [can] we begin to fuse our powers."[13] Here and there, academics, activists, and concerned citizens from a remarkable rainbow of ethnic and economic backgrounds are merging their skills, their voices, and their very differences in shrewd, united strategies designed to transform our environments.

BUILDING WOMEN-SUPPORTING NEIGHBORHOODS

Gilman's architectural dream of domestic liberty for all, accomplished through the unified construction of neighborhoods, is taking tangible form today in many parts of the United States and Canada.[14] At scattered sites in at least thirty-six states and Puerto Rico, grass-roots activists in this country are joining forces with building professionals and other sympathizers to translate the housing needs and dreams of particular groups of women into built form. Funneling different strengths to the process, such coalitions are held together by a common commitment to the material empowerment of women, starting with the least advantaged.

Aroused by the diminishing supply of affordable housing, many secular and religious groups and alliances have recently become galvanized around the human right to decent housing. Drawing fiscal support from a combination of private and public sources (via national, state, and local agencies), impressively determined networks have coalesced for several related purposes: to care for the growing stream of homeless individuals, to develop permanent affordable housing units, to build housing that supports the needs of women, and to advocate for fair and reasonable housing policies. Bertha Gilkey and the public housing tenants she has organized in St. Louis, the housing and economic development partnership of Dolores Hayden and Ena Dubnoff in Los Angeles, the Roman Catholic Sisters of Mercy, located throughout the United States, concentrating particularly in Philadelphia and Baltimore, and the Women's Institute for Housing and Economic Development, now in Boston, are just a few of the many individuals and groups currently struggling, on a day-to-day basis, to unite a vision of feminist architecture with actual building programs linking residential units with coordinated domestic services and jobs.[15]

From her vantage point early in this century, Charlotte Gilman could not foresee the complexity of the challenge of actually building socialized

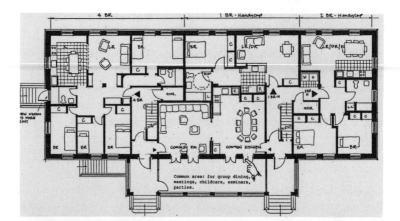

Proposed design for the rehabilitation of Greenpoint Hospital (Brooklyn, New York), to include thirty-seven units of housing for women and single parents. Project of the National Congress of Neighborhood Women, Katrin Adam and Barbara Marks, architects. Intergenerational housing connecting community spaces, private dwellings, and shared domestic facilities has many benefits for people of all ages. Photograph of residents of St. Clair O'Connor Community, a project of the Mennonite Church in Toronto, Ontario, Canada. Photo courtesy of the *Toronto Star*.

neighborhoods that would enhance the racial, economic, and gender democracy in this country. Little did she know that the cost of auxiliary social buildings (or rooms) would appear to most people to be prohibitive. Nor did she understand how to locate and cultivate appropriate constituencies. Instead of the rallying cry for progressive coalitions, her indiscriminate cheering for "Growth, glorious Growth" was coopted as a theme song both by profit-obsessed real estate developers and by multinational corporations, voraciously in search of increasing markets around the world.

On other matters, Gilman was more perceptive. She recognized that women's ability to pay for housing is directly linked to their having good jobs; both housing and economic opportunities for women are linked necessities, and the more closely integrated the better. In her ideal visions, the worlds of work and family have been reconciled and united, both socially and spatially, and that image is an inspiration for days to come. She appreciated the threat to her architectural vision posed by excessive military spending, anticipating the ominous way in which a multibillion dollar annual "Star Wars" appropriation could and does sabotage the orderly investment of public funds in programs that address genuine human needs, such as housing, women-supporting domestic services, and economic development.

Gilman's portrait of alternative neighborhood designs still has enough vitality to engage dreamer/builders suggestively today. Her imaginary apartment buildings, for example, with hotel-sized kitchens, dining and social rooms, provide their occupants with enviable convenience, social access to each other, and privacy. Likewise, her representation of child-care facilities serving families in a particular geographical cluster has an exemplary appeal. In several cases, the places found in Gilman's fiction are dynamic enough to invite contemporary imitation.

People who are taking up the present challenge of building supportive domestic and work environments find that they must address many important practical questions of which Gilman was unaware. Which particular groups will combine forces to design and build socialized neighborhoods and actually live in them, for example? Who will do the organizing of these groups? Once a coalition is formed, who will nurture the new organizational entity? Who will do the shared domestic work? Who will wash the dishes? How can we promote democratic domesticity, in which males as well as females learn to take repsonsibility for their own daily needs . . . and mess? Which domestic services can best be done cooperatively and which commercially? Can funding sources be found which can sustain the additional expense of common spaces and services? Is adequate funding more likely to come from state agencies or private corporations?

Gilman wrote the long poem, "The Burden of Mothers: A Clarion Call to Redeem the Race" sometime during the 1890s. The two verses that appear as this chapter's epigraph are the first and the last of its seventeen verses. The intervening verses illustrate the penchant she had for shooting herself in the foot, calling for heroic altruism and no self-interest from the oppressed mothers of "a stumbling world."

Despite her excessive expectations of women to be self-sacrificing, Gilman took a significant step in consciousness between the first and last stanzas of her early elegy. The first verse appeals, in an altruistic, social service mode, to "your ages of anguish," "your sorrow," and "your pain," as if "the burden of mothers" was a bond seen from an elevated, superior vantage point above "their" conflict and distress.

By the time she got to the seventeenth verse, however, she had dropped the pretense of exteriority and claimed a share of "the burden" for herself. The lines had become transformed into "our ages of anguish," "our sorrow," and "our pain." She thereby replaced the third person with a more poignant first-person voice. By poem's end, she was calling, out of her own pain and anger, for the empowerment of herself and her sisters. Instead of a vertical, trickle-down model of social change, she here left us with a horizontal, democratic validation of her own experience and that of other women. She began to look squarely at the diverse pain and anger of women and see that it could become a shared capacity to exert political power. Within that transformation lie the seeds of a process by which people can learn not only to dream about but also to construct for themselves real environments that effectively enhance the domestic liberty of their inhabitants.

Notes

INTRODUCTION

1 · Gilman, *The Home: Its Work and Influence* (McClure, Phillips, 1903; reprint ed., Urbana: University of Illinois Press, 1972), p. 12.

2 · Gilman, "All the World to Her," *Independent,* July 9, 1903, pp. 1614–15.

3 · Gilman, *The Living of Charlotte Perkins Gilman: An Autobiography* (Appleton-Century, 1935; reprint ed., New York: Arno Press, 1972), p. 332.

4 · Ibid., pp. 99, 103.

1. THE SOCIAL LANDSCAPE IN GILMAN'S DAY

1 · E P. Thompson, *The Making of the English Working Class* (Harmondsworth: Penguin Books, 1968), p. 445.

2 · Alice Kessler-Harris, *Out to Work: A History of Wage-Earning Women in the United States* (Oxford: Oxford University Press, 1982), p. 18.

3 · Mari Jo Buhle, *Women and American Socialism, 1870–1920* (Urbana: University of Illinois Press, 1983), p. 30.

4 · Kessler-Harris, *Out to Work,* pp. 22–23.

5 · Kessler-Harris reports that 4,200,000 immigrants entered the United States between 1840 and 1860. Ibid., p. 47.

6 · Mary P. Ryan, *Cradle of the Middle Class: The Family in Oneida County, New York, 1790–1865* (Cambridge: Cambridge University Press, 1981), pp. 232–34.

7 · In her richly detailed historical study of household work before, during, and after industrialization, Ruth Schwartz Cowan illustrates the gender mutuality and interdependence of preindustrial domesticity. "The daily exigencies of agrarian life," she writes, "meant that men and women had to work in tandem in order to undertake any single life-sustaining chore." *More Work for Mother: The Ironies of Household Technology from the Open Hearth to the Microwave* (New York: Basic Books, 1983), p. 38 et passim.

8 · In *Out to Work,* Kessler-Harris points out that modern household technology was a "double-edged sword" because, "in reducing the need for domestic help, it placed the entire burden of household maintenance on the shoulders of one woman, enhancing her isolation within a private household" (pp. 111–13).

Besides ably documenting the same point, Cowan has demonstrated that, although modern technology has removed much household drudgery, it has replaced many arduous systems of labor with modern ones that often take as much time as (sometimes more than) the old ones did. See *More Work for Mother,* pp. 63–65 et passim.

9 · Susan Strasser, *Never Done: The History of American Housework* (New York: Pantheon Books, 1983), p. 29. Cowan points out that ordinary people, before the twentieth century, ate a very simple, unvaried diet. *More Work for Mother,* p. 21 et passim.

10 · Kessler Harris, *Out to Work,* p. 112.

11 · Ibid., pp. 120–21.

12 · Ibid. p. 49.

13 · See Barbara Welter's classic discussion of ideological change concerning women and the home during the Industrial Revolution, "The Cult of True Womanhood, 1820–1860," *American Quarterly,* Summer 1966.

14 · Kathryn Kish Sklar, *Catharine Beecher: A Study in American Domesticity* (New York: W. W. Norton, 1973), p. 113.

15 · Ryan, *Cradle of the Middle Class,* p. 232.

16 · Kessler-Harris, *Out to Work,* p. 53.

17 · Philippe Aries, *Centuries of Childhood: A Social History of Family Life* (New York: Vintage Books, 1962), p. 415.

18 · Ryan, chapter title in *Cradle of the Middle Class.*

19 · Buhle, *Women and American Socialism,* p. 62 et passim.

20 · Ibid., pp. 53, 56.

21 · Karen J. Blair, *The Clubwoman As Feminist: True Womanhood Redefined, 1868–1914* (New York: Holmes and Meier, 1980), p. 119 et passim.

22 · Mary Hill reports that 80 percent of colleges and universities had begun admitting women by 1900. *Charlotte Perkins Gilman: The Making of a Radical Feminist, 1860–1986* (Philadelphia: Temple University Press, 1980), p. 179.

23 · Dolores Hayden, *The Grand Domestic Revolution: A History of Feminist Designs for American Homes, Neighborhoods, and Cities* (Cambridge, Mass.: MIT Press, 1981), p. 3 et passim. In light of her richly detailed and thoughtful account, Dolores Hayden can quite properly be described as the biographer of an important social conception in American life. Having located written sources and drawings for innumerable historical episodes comprising a material feminist tradition, Hayden has reconstructed a substantial community of nineteenth-century detractors from the popular notion of two distinct gender spheres, dissenters who shared an architectural perspective. Composed of journalists, utopian novelists, socialists, anarchists, suffragists, home economists, and social workers, this reform community concurred that the social and physical environment of domestic work was in urgent need of democratic rearrangement.

24 · Ibid., pp. 33–35.

25 · Ibid., pp. 77–82 et passim.

26 · Ibid., p. 95.

27 · Ibid., pp. 108, 91, 103.

28 · Ibid., p. 60.

29 · Ibid., p. 117.

30 · Ibid., pp. 165, 174. See also Kathryn Kish Sklar, "Hull House in the 1890s: A Community of Women Reformers," *Signs* 10 (Summer 1985): 658–77.

31 · Hayden, *Grand Domestic Revolution,* pp. 135–49.

32 · Buhle, *Women and American Socialism,* p. 77 et passim.

33 · Edward Bellamy, *Looking Backward,* (New York: New American Library, 1960), pp. 45, 99.

2. WHO WAS CHARLOTTE PERKINS GILMAN?

1 · The awkwardness of nomenclature in this book illustrates the identity disadvantage women suffer in this society. Née Charlotte Anna Perkins in 1860, our subject married Charles Walter Stetson in 1884 and used the name Stetson until 1900 despite the early dissolution of that marriage. On June 11, 1900, she married George Houghton Gilman (her cousin) and thereafter went by the name of Charlotte Perkins Gilman. Although she frequently championed the right of married women to retain their own names and admired Lucy Stone for pioneering on that issue, our subject was not particularly attached to the name Perkins and chose to use her husbands' names. She lived longest with the name Gilman (thirty-five years) and is best known by that name. Therefore, to enhance the coherence of her story, the subject of this book will be referred to in the text as Gilman, even when doing so is anachronistic. Were she a male author, there would be no such conundrum.

2 · Gilman, *Living,* pp. 186–87.

3 · Ibid., p. 247.

4 · Ibid., p. 335.

5 · Quoted in "Foreword" to ibid., p. xviii.

6 · Ibid., p. 267.

7 · Hill, *Charlotte Gilman,* pp. 45, 229, 288–89n.

8 · Ibid., p. 112.

9 · Gilman, *Living,* pp. 12–13, 27, 18. Mary Hill notes that four years of formal schooling was "still the average" in the 1870s. *Charlotte Gilman,* p. 41.

10 · Gilman, *Living,* pp. 7–8.

11 · Hill, *Charlotte Gilman,* p. 36.

12 · Gilman, *Living,* pp. 28, 68, 67.

13 · Ibid., p. 27.

14 · Ibid., p. 39.

15 · Ibid., pp. 328, 40.

16 · Gilman, *The Science of Human Conduct,* p. 216, in Gilman Papers, The Stowe, Beecher, Hooker, Seymour, Day Memorial Library and Historical Foundtion, Nook Farm Research Library, Hartford, Conn.

17 · Gilman, *In This Our World,* 3rd ed. (Boston: Small, Maynard, 1908), pp. 48–49.

18 · Gilman, *Living,* p. 59.

19 · Ibid., p. 83.

20 · When discussing Gilman's marriages, the identity disadvantage women suffer is particularly nettlesome.

21 · Gilman, *Living,* p. 92.

22 · Ibid., p. 95.

23 · Ibid., p. 96.

24 · Ibid., p. 111.

25 · Quoted in Hill, *Charlotte Gilman,* p. 200.

26 · Gilman, *Living,* p. 162.

27 · Helen Campbell, *Household Ecnomics: A Course in Household Science* (New York: G. P. Putnam's Sons, 1896), p. 37.

28 · Buhle, *Women and American Socialism,* p. 79.

29 · "Similar Cases" can also be found in Gilman's book of poetry, *In This Our World,* p. 95.

30 · Gilman, *Living,* pp. 166–67.

31 · Aileen Kraditor, *The Ideas of the Woman Suffrage Movement, 1890–1920* (Garden City, N.Y.: Doubleday [Anchor Books], 1971), pp. 68–69.

32 · Gilman, *Living,* p. 121; see also Gilman, "Why I Wrote The Yellow Wallpaper," *Forerunner* 4 (October 1913): 271. Throughout her life, Gilman suffered periodic bouts of acute depression. In 1901 she met a "remarkable" doctor in New York City, Mary Putnam Jacobi, who treated Gilman's ailment for several months, a course of treatment that the patient reported "did me much good." See Gilman, *Living,* p. 291.

33 · Gilman, *Living,* p. 169.

34 · Ibid., p. 237.

35 · David Allen Shannon, *The Socialist Party of America* (Chicago: Quadrangle Books, 1967); and Sara Evans, *Personal Politics: The Roots of Women's Liberation in the Civil Rights Movement and the New Left* (New York: Random House [Vintage Books], 1980), p. 105.

36 · Gilman, "The Socialist and the Suffragist," last two of six verses, *Life and Labor* 2 (February 1912): 61; also in *Forerunner* 1 (Oct. 1910): 25.

37 · Gilman, *Forerunner* 2 (May 1911): 124.

38 · Gilman, "A Summary of Purpose," *Forerunner* 7 (November 1916): 286–87. Although its subscription list never reached 3,000, Madeleine Stern has estimated that the *Forerunner's* regular readership included 5,000 to 7,000 people, calculated on the implied basis of library subscriptions and informal sharing

among friends. Distributed by suffrage and socialist groups as well as the Rand School of Social Science, the journal was not for sale at newsstands. Rudolph Rochow, himself a subscriber, was the magazine's printer; the Charlton Company on Wall Street, the name of which was made by combining "Charlotte" and "Houghton," was its publisher. See Madeleine B. Stern, "The Forerunner," in *The American Radical Press, 1880–1960,* ed. Joseph R. Conlin, 2 vols. (Westport, Conn.: Greenwood Press, 1974), 2: 439 et passim. Stern's essay also appears as the introduction to Greenwood Press's reprint edition of *The Forerunner* (New York: Greenwood Press, 1968), vol. 1, unpaginated.

39 · Gilman, *Forerunner* 1 (November 1909): 32.

40 · Judith Schwarz, *Radical Feminists of Heterodoxy* (Norwich, Vt: New Victoria Publishers, 1986), pp. 28–29 et passim.

41 · Kraditor, *Woman Suffrage Movement,* pp. 192–93. See also Eleanor Flexner, *Century of Struggle: The Woman's Rights Movement in the United States,* rev. ed. (Cambridge, Mass.: Harvard University Press [Belknap Press], 1975), pp. 271–85.

42 · As an older woman, Gilman was decidedly more straitlaced on matters sexual than she had been earlier. There is some evidence to suggest that she enjoyed several sexual relationships outside of her two marriages, both with women and with men. See in particular Hill's discussion of Gilman's friendships with Martha Luther, Delle Knapp, Edwin Markham, and Eugene Hough, in *Charlotte Gilman;* and Schwartz's conjectures in *Heterodoxy,* p. 85 et passim.

43 · Gilman, "A Suggestion on the Negro Problem," *American Journal of Sociology* 14 (July 1908): 78–85.

44 · Gilman, "The Passing of Matrimony," *Harper's Bazaar* 40 (June 1906): 498.

45 · Gilman, *Living,* p. 252.

46 · Kraditor, *Woman Suffrage Movement,* p. 113. See also the *Proceedings of the 35th Annual Convention of the National-American Woman Suffrage Association* (Warren, Ohio: Wm. Ritezel, 1903), p. 43, for reference to Gilman's speech, entitled "Educated Suffrage A Fetich."

47 · Gilman, "Race Pride," *Forerunner* 4 (April 1913): 89, 90.

48 · Gilman, *With Her in Ourland,* in *Forerunner* 7 (June 1916): 156.

49 · Gilman, "Comment," *Forerunner* 7 (September 1916): 251–52.

50 · Gilman, *Women and Economics,* p. 78.

51 · Gilman, *Living,* pp. 183.

52 · Ibid., pp. 333, 334.

53 · Gilman, "Good and Bad Taste in Suicide," *Forerunner* 3 (May 1912): 130.

3. GILMAN'S ATTENTION TO DOMESTIC ARCHITECTURE

1 · Gilman, *Living,* p. 294.

2 · Ibid., p. 283.

3 · Gilman, *The Home,* p. 114.

4 · Gilman, *Women and Economics,* pp. 238, 267.

5 · Gilman, *Pernicious Adam,* chap. 24, unpublished manuscript in Gilman Papers, Schlesinger Library. Because the pagination is incomplete and irregular, reference is made only to chapter.

6 · Gilman, *The Home,* p. 36.

7 · Gilman, *Women and Economics,* p. 203.

8 · Gilman, "Why Cooperative Housekeeping Fails," *Harper's Bazaar* 41 (July 1907): 627.

9 · Gilman, *In This Our World,* p. 160. (A hod is a coal scuttle.)

10 · Gilman, *The Home,* p. 311.

11 · Gilman, "The Beauty of a Block," *Independent,* Summer 1909, (hand dated by Gilman), p. 70; in Gilman Papers, Schlesinger Library.

12 · Gilman, *The Home,* p. 315.

13 · Gilman, "Domestic Economy," *Independent* 10, no. 2 (no date): 1359; in Gilman Papers, Schlesinger Library.

14 · Gilman, *Women and Economics,* p. 243.

15 · Gilman, "Does a Man Support His Wife?" *Forerunner* 2 (Spetember 1911): 243.

16 · Gilman, *The Home,* pp. 117, 98–100.

17 · Ibid., pp. 118–19, 52.

18 · Gilman, "The Kitchen-Fly," *Forerunner* 1 (August 1910): 8.

19 · Gilman, "The Home without a Kitchen," *Puritan,* n.d. (dated 1900 in author's hand), in Gilman Papers, Schlesinger Library, p. 417.

20 · Gilman, *The Home,* p. 83.

21 · Ibid., p. 281.

22 · Gilman, "The Family in Modern Society" (ca. 1908) p. 16; in Gilman Papers, Schlesinger Library.

23 · Gilman, *Women and Economics,* pp. 246–47.

24 · Gilman, *Our Androcentric Culture,* in *Forerunner* 1 (December 1909): 22.

25 · Gilman, *The Home,* p. 151.

26 · Ibid., pp. 152, 275.

27 · Ibid., p. 291.

28 · Ibid., pp. 297, 326.

29 · Gilman, *Women and Economics,* pp. 268, 168.

30 · Gilman, "Genius, Domestic and Maternal," *Forerunner* 1 (June 1910): 10.

31 · Gilman, *Pernicious Adam,* chap. 25.

32 · Gilman, *Human Work* (New York: McClure, Phillips, 1904), p. 151.

33 · Gilman, *Women and Economics,* p. 120.

34 · Gilman, *The Home,* p. 274.

35 · Gilman, *Forerunner* 3 (September 1912): 247.

36 · Gilman, *The Home,* p. 275.

37 · Gilman, *Forerunner* 3 (September 1912): 248–49.

38 · Gilman, *Forerunner* 1 (September 1910): 18.

39 · Gilman, *Pernicious Adam,* chap. 25.

40 · Gilman, "The Future of the Home," *Independent,* n.d., p. 791, Gilman Papers, Schlesinger Library.

41 · Gilman, *The Home,* pp. 311, 315.

42 · Ibid., p. 13, 319, et passim.

43 · Gilman, *Pernicious Adam,* chap. 24.

44 · Gilman, *Women and Economics,* pp. 219–20.

45 · Gilman, *The Home,* p. 277.

46 · Ibid., pp. 100–101.

47 · Gilman, *Concerning Children* (Boston: Small, Maynard, and Company, 1900), p. 197.

48 · Ibid.

49 · Gilman, "Looking and Seeing," *Forerunner* 2 (December 1911): 328.

50 · Gilman, Private Morality and Public Immorality," *Forerunner* 1 (January 1910): 9.

51 · Gilman, *Science of Human Conduct,* p. 25. Chap. 15, "Unnamed Crimes," discusses the nature of social wrong.

52 · See "Two Callings," one of Gilman's favorites among her own poems, quoted as frontispiece to *The Home.*

53 · Gilman, *Women and Economics,* pp. 280–81.

54 · The phrase is attributed to Elise Boulding by Gerda Wekerle, in *New Spaces for Women,* ed. Wekerle, R. Peterson, and D. Morley (Boulder, Colo.: Westview Press, 1980), p. 28.

4. GILMAN'S UTOPIAN PORTRAIT OF NONSEXIST LANDSCAPES

1 · Gilman, "Thoughts and Figgerings," 1893, unpublished notebook-diary, Gilman Papers, Schlesinger Library.

2 · Dolores Hayden, "Catherine Beecher and the Politics of Housework," in *Women in American Architecture: A Historical and Contemporary Perpective,* ed. Susanna Torre (New York: Watson & Guptill, 1977), p. 43.

3 · Gilman, *Women and Economics,* pp. 161–63.

4 · Hayden, *Grand Domestic Revolution,* p. 185.

5 · Hayden, "Redesigning the Domestic Workplace," in *New Space for Women,* ed. Wekerle et al, p. 105.

6 · August Bebel, *Woman under Socialism* (New York: Schocken Books, 1971; reprinted from the N.Y. Labor News Press ed. of 1904), p. 340.

7 · Gilman, *Living,* p. 201.

8 · Gilman, *The Home,* pp. 339–40, and *Living,* p. 252.

9 · *Moving the Mountain* (New York: Charlton) was also published as a separate

volume in 1911. *Herland* first appeared on its own in 1979 when Ann J. Lane published a reprint edition (New York: Pantheon Books).

10 · See Ann Lane's "Introduction" to *Herland,* p. xix.

11 · Vernon Louis Parrington, Jr., *American Dreams: A Study of American Utopias* (New York: Russell & Russell, 1964), p. 57 et passim.

12 · *Moving the Mountain,* in *Forerunner* 2 (February 1911): 56.

13 · Ibid. (July 1911): 195.

14 · Ibid. (August 1911): 220.

15 · *Herland,* ed. Ann J. Lane, pp. 11, 18, 19.

16 · Ibid., p. 98.

17 · Ibid., p. 137.

18 · Ibid., pp. 54–57, 69.

19 · *With Her in Ourland,* in *Forerunner* 7 (March, May 1915): 69, 125.

20 · *Moving the Mountain,* in *Forerunner* 2 (March, July, November 1911): 79, 194, 307.

21 · Ibid. (June 1911): 165.

5. GILMAN'S PRAGMATIC APPROACH TO NEIGHBORHOOD DESIGN

1 · Gilman, *Women and Economics,* p. 242.

2 · Gilman, "Homes without House Keeping: A Present Demand," in *Delineator,* May 1907, p. 876.

3 · Gilman, "The Best for the Poorest," reprinted in *Forerunner* 7 (October 1916): 260–62.

4 · Gilman, "Beauty of a Block," p. 67.

5 · Ibid., p. 70.

6 · Ibid.

7 · Ibid., pp. 71–72.

8 · Gilman, *Women and Economics,* p. 243.

9 · Gilman, "Applepieville," *Independent,* September 25, 1920.

10 · Gilman, "Domestic Economy."

11 · Gilman, *The Home,* p. 334; see also "Why Cooperative Housekeeping Fails," p. 629.

12 · Gilman, "The Best for the Poorest," p. 262.

13 · Gilman, "Why Cooperative Housekeeping Fails," p. 628.

14 · Gilman, "Home without a Kitchen," p. 421.

15 · Gilman, "Why Cooperative Housekeeping Fails," p. 628.

16 · Gilman, "Genius, Domestic and Maternal," pt. 2, *Forerunner* 1 (July 1910): 5.

17 · Gilman, *Concerning Children,* p. 130.

18 · Ibid., p. 124.

19 · Gilman, "Genius, Domestic and Maternal," pt. 2, p. 5.

20 · Gilman, *Moving the Mountain,* in *Forerunner* 2 (August 1911): 223.

21 · Gilman, *With Her in Ourland,* in *Forerunner* 7 (September 1916): 241; (July 1916): 184–85 et passim.

6. GILMAN'S PHILOSOPHY OF WORLD IMPROVEMENT
LED BY WOMEN

1 · Gilman, "Toward Monogamy," in *Our Changing Morality,* ed. Freda Kirchwey (New York: Albert and Charles Boni, 1924), p. 61.

2 · Gilman, "Selfishness and Socialism," *American Fabian* 4 (April 1898).

3 · Gilman, *Living,* p. 154.

4 · Published works: *Human Work* (1904); *Our Brains and What Ails Them* (1912); *Humanness* (1913); *Social Ethics* (1914); *Growth and Combat* (1916); *His Religion and Hers* (1923). Unpublished works: *Pernicious Adam* (1931); three versions of *The Science of Human Conduct* (1930s, undated).

5 · Gilman, *Human Work,* p. 134.

6 · Gilman, *Social Ethics,* in *Forerunner* 5 (January 1914): 23.

7 · Charles W. Eliot, *The Conflict between Individualism and Collectivism in a Democracy* (New York: Charles Scribner's Sons, 1912), p. 1.

8 · Gilman, *Human Work,* chap. 4.

9 · Gilman, *Pernicious Adam,* p. 140.

10 · Quoted in "Foreword" to Gilman, *Living,* p. xxi.

11 · Gilman, *His Religion and Hers: A Study of the Faith of Our Fathers and the Work of Our Mothers* (New York: Century, 1923), pp. 243, 247.

12 · Gilman, "Our Overworked Instincts," *Forerunner* 1 (December 1910): 13.

13 · Gilman, *Social Ethics,* in *Forerunner* 5 (January 1914): 20.

14 · Gilman, *The Home,* pp. 16–17, 23.

15 · Gilman, "A Moving Faith," *Forerunner* 3 (October 1912): 259.

16 · Gilman, *Social Ethics,* in *Forerunner* 5 (May 1914): 135–36.

17 · Gilman, *His Religion and Hers,* p. 297.

18 · Gilman, *The Science of Human Conduct,* p. 237; "The Real Truth in Christianty," *Forerunner* 3 (May 1912): 118; *His Religion and Hers,* pp. 12, 14.

19 · Gilman, *The Home,* p. 25.

20 · Gilman, *Living,* p. 331.

21 · Sir Patrick Geddes and J. Arthur Thomson, *The Evolution of Sex* (New York: Scribner and Welford, 1890), p. 50.

22 · Ibid., p. 271.

23 · Ibid., p. 267.

24 · Gilman, *Living,* p. 259.

25 · Gilman, review of Ward, *Pure Sociology,* in *Forerunner* 1 (October 1910): 26.

26 · Lester Frank Ward, "Our Better Halves," *Forum* 6 (November 1888): 266.

27 · Gilman, "Woman, the Enigma," *Harper's Bazaar,* December 1908: p. 1193.

28 · Ann Douglas Wood, " 'The Fashionable Diseases': Women's Complaints and Their Treatment in Nineteenth Century America," in *Clio's Consciousness Raised,* ed. Mary S. Hartman and Lois Banner (New York: Harper and Row, 1974), p. 3.

29 · Gilman, *Living,* p. 67.

30 · Gilman, *The Dress of Women,* in *Forerunner* 6 (March 1915): 79–81.

31 · Gilman, *Women and Economics,* p. 59.

32 · Gilman, "That Obvious Purpose," *Forerunner* 2 (June 1911): 162.

33 · Gilman, *Our Brains and What Ails Them,* in *Forerunner* 3 (December 1912): 334.

34 · Gilman, *The Home,* pp. 313–14.

35 · Gilman, "What Are 'Feminine' Qualities," *Forerunner* 5 (September 1914): 233.

36 · Gilman, "The Humanness of Women," *Forerunner* 1 (January 1910): 12.

37 · Gilman, *Forerunner* 5 (September 1914): 225.

7. THE POWER OF GILMAN'S STORYTELLING VOICE

1 · Gilman "The Editor's Problem," *Forerunner* 1 (August 1910): 24. All the stories discussed in this chapter were published in the *Forerunner,* starting (except in one instance) on p. 1.

2 · Quoted in Alexander Black, "The Woman Who Saw It First," *Century Magazine* 85 (November 1923): 39.

3 · Gilman, "Thoughts and Figgerings," December 1926.

4 · *Forerunner* 4 (January 1913).

5 · *Forerunner* 1 (January 1910).

6 · *Forerunner* 1 (April 1910).

7 · In addition to her appearance here, Benigna MacAvelly is the central character in a novel bearing her name, as well as an important supporting figure in both a second novel and at least seven short stories. *Benigna MacAvelly* was published serially in the 1914 *Forerunner,* vol. 5; likewise, the second novel, *Won Over,* appeared in the 1913 *Forerunner,* vol. 4. MacAvelly also figures in the following short stories published in the *Forerunner:* in vol. 1, "According to Solomon" (December 1909), "Martha's Mother" (April 1910), and "A Coincidence" (July 1910); in vol. 2, "Mrs. Potter and the Clay Club" (February 1911); in vol. 3, "Mrs. Elder's Idea" (February 1912), "An Innocent Girl" (March 1912), and "Maidstone Comfort" (September 1912). Gilman's delight in a fictional

character whose name suggests that good ends justify morally questionable means illustrates the evil-denying flaw in her vision, discussed in chap. 6.

8 · *Forerunner* 3 (August 1912).

9 · *Forerunner* 3 (October 1912).

10 · *Forerunner* 2 (December 1911).

11 · *Forerunner* 2 (November 1911).

12 · *Forerunner* 1 (August 1910).

13 · *Forerunner* 4 (August 1913); 7 (May 1916).

14 · *Forerunner* 4 (April 1913).

15 · *Forerunner* 1 (November 1909).

16 · *Forerunner* 6 (May 1915).

17 · *Forerunner* 3 (September 1912).

18 · *Forerunner* 2, (April 1911).

19 · *Forerunner* 6 (June 1915).

20 · Stanley Hauerwas, "The Self as Story: Religion and Morality from the Agent's Perspective," *Journal of Religious Ethics* 1 (Fall 1973): 76.

8. CONCLUSION

1 · Hayden, *Grand Domestic Revolution*. Within Hayden's four chapters, entitled "Charlotte Perkins Gilman and Her Influence," see pp. 197–200, 242–48.

2 · Ibid., pp. 262–63 et passim, and chap. 10 (pp. 206–27).

3 · Gwendolyn Wright, *Building the Dream: A Social History of Housing in America* (Cambridge, Mass.: MIT Press, 1983), p. 205–7.

4 · Ibid., pp. 222–25.

5 · Dolores Hayden, *Redesigning the American Dream: The Future of Housing, Work, and Family Life* (New York: W. W. Norton, 1984). pp. 1–12.

6 · Ellen Perry Berkeley, "The Swedish 'servicehus,'" *Architecture Plus*, May 1973, p. 56.

7 · Hayden, *Redesigning the American Dream*, pp. 163, 137 et passim.

8 · Gilman, *Social Ethics*, in *Forerunner* 5 (February 1914): 48.

9 · Gilman, "A Side View," *Forerunner* 5 (August 1914): 213.

10 · See, in particular, Gilman, *Women and Economics*, chap. 7 (pp. 128–29 et passim).

11 · Adrienne Rich, "Disloyal to Civilization: Feminism, Racism, Gynephobia" in *On Lies, Secrets, and Silence* (New York: W. W. Norton, 1979), pp. 299–300, 285 et passim.

12 · Audre Lorde, "The Master's Tools Will Never Dismantle the Master's House," in *This Bridge Called My Back: Writings By Radical Women of Color*, ed. Cherríe Moraga and Gloria Anzaldúa (Watertown, Mass.: Persephone Press, 1981), p. 99.

13 · Rich, *On Lies*, p. 299.

14 · A quarterly newsletter, *Women and Environments* (c/o Centre for Urban and Community Studies, 455 Spadina Avenue, Toronto, Ontario, Canada M5S2G8) is an excellent networking, informational resource for learning of similar projects in the larger national and international context.

15 · The National Congress of Neighborhood Women, a coalition of grass-roots organizations with national headquarters in Brooklyn, New York, has taken an important leadership role in developing supportive means of communication and resource sharing among community-based groups concerned with women's housing strategies. In October 1987 it sponsored an international/national conference in Camden, New Jersey, on Housing Options for Women. For information, contact NCNW, 249 Manhattan Ave., Brooklyn, New York 12111.

Index

Abel, Mary Hinman, 23
Addams, Jane, 20, 39, 60, 85, 131
American Fabian, 43
American Sociological Society, 133
Andrews, Stephen Pearl, 22
Anthony, Susan B., 17
Atlantic Monthly, 23
Austin, Alice Constance, 169

Bachofen, Johann Jakob, 134
Baldwin Hill Village, Calif., 170
Balitmore, Md., 175
Barrie, Eleanor, ix
Bebel, August, 84–85
Beecher, Catharine, 15–16, 22, 30, 32
Beecher, Henry Ward, 30
Beecher (Hooker), Isabella, 30, 32
Beecher, Lyman, 30
Beecher (Perkins), Mary, 31–32
Beecher family, 11–13, 22–23, 30, 31–
    32, 39, 57, 83–84
"Bee Wise," 88, 93–96, 99–102, 117
Bellamy, Edward, 24–25, 86, 89, 117,
    130
Boston, Mass., 23, 24–25, 32, 84, 110,
    175
Brown University, 133
"Burden of Mothers, The: A Clarion
    Call to Redeem the Race," 165, 178
Burns, Lucy, 50

Cambridge, Mass., viii, 22, 37
Cambridge Cooperative Housekeeping
    Society, 22, 63

Campbell, Helen (Weeks), 41, 59, 60,
    85
Capitalism: Bellamy's critique of, 86;
    and industrialization, 11–13; and re-
    sistance to CPG's program, 77–78;
    softened state capitalism à la CPG,
    115–17
Carl Mackley Houses, 170
Catt, Carrie Chapman, 43
Chamberlin, Dorothy Stetson, viii
Channing (Stetson), Grace Ellery, 37–
    39, 40, 54
Channing family, 38, 39, 59
Charlton Company, 21, 183 n.38, 185
    n.9
Chatauqua, N.Y., 85
Child care: Bebel's plans for, 84–85;
    CPG's alternative designs for, 106–7,
    112–14, 115; CPG's critique of exist-
    ing, 73–74; in CPG's realistic stories,
    149–51, 152–53; in CPG's utopian
    stories, 90–92, 94, 98; Fourier's and
    Owen's designs for, 20
City Housing Corporation, 169–70
*Cityless and Countryless World: An Outline of
    Practical Cooperative Individualism*
    (Olerich), 24
"City's Beauty," 9, 41
Claflin, Tenn., 23
"Cleared Path, A," 151–52
Concerning Children, 112–14
Congregate housing, 168, 176
Congressional Union. *See* National
    Woman's party

"Cottagette, The," 153–55, 163
"Council of War, A," 155–57

Darrow, Clarence, 47
Darwin, Charles, 25
Diaz, Abby Morton, 24
Diothas, The: or A Far Look Ahead
    (Macnie), 89
Dorr, Rheta Childe, 49
"Dr. Clair's Place," 160–62
Dubnoff, Ena, 175

Eastman, Crystal, 49
Eliot, Charles, 125
Environmentalism (ecology), 86, 90, 94,
    99–100
Eugenics, 18, 96, 101–2, 125
Evolution of Sex (Geddes), 131–33

Fabian Society, 43, 122
Family wage, 71
Feminism, nineteenth and early twen-
    tieth century: architectural, 5–7; ar-
    chitectural, in CPG's stories, 145–69;
    CPG's blend of socialism and, 29–31,
    47–50; CPG's critique of conven-
    tional domesticity, 66–71; CPG's
    philosophical perspective compared
    to her architectural one, 121, 171–
    75; importance of anger and subjec-
    tivity to, 178; material, 20–25, 84–
    85
Feminist Alliance, 168
Food delivery: Bebel's plans for, 84;
    CPG's critique of conventional, 64–
    66; CPG's program for, 106–7, 109–
    13; portrayed in CPG's realistic
    stories, 115, 147, 151, 153–55; por-
    trayed in utopian fiction, 90–92, 94,
    98; in settlement houses and resorts,
    85
Forerunner, The, 6, 48–49, 87, 88, 114,
    145, 188 n.1
"Forsythe and Forsythe," 146–47
Fourier, Charles, 20–23, 84–85
Freudianism, 50

Gale, Zona, 49
Garland, Hamlin, 44
Geddes, Sir Patrick, 131–34, 139–40
Gender ideology, 15–16, 136–40
Geography of gender, 5–6
Gilkey, Bertha, 175
Gilman, George Houghton, 45, 49, 51,
    54, 59, 156
"Girls and the Land," 159
Griffith, Mary, 89
Gynaecocentrism, 133–35

Hale, Edward Everett, 41, 84
Hartford, Conn., viii, 31, 33
Harvard University, viii, ix, 125
Hauerwas, Stanley, 163
Hayden, Dolores, viii, 20, 175, 180 n.23
Hearst newspapers, 41
"Her Housekeeper," 147–48, 163
Herland, 88, 96–102, 116
"Her Memories," 149–51
Heterodoxy, 49, 168–69
Higginson, Thomas Wentworth, 47
Hill, Mary, 30, 32, 183 n.42
"Holy Stove, The," 62
"Housewife, The," 69–70
Howard, Ebenezer, 169
Howe, Julia Ward, 17
Howe, Marie Jenney, 49–50, 126
Howells, William Dean, 24, 41, 44
Howes, Ethel Puffer, 169
Howland, Marie Stevens, 23, 24, 85
Hubert, Philip G., 22–23
Hubert Home Clubs, 23
Hull House (Chicago), 42, 85

Impress, 41
Individualism, 123–25
Institute for the Coordination of
    Women's Interests, 169
Intercollegiate Socialist, 47
Intercollegiate Socialist Society, 47
In This Our World, 44
Irving, Washington, 89
Israel, 170

James, William, 131
Johnson, Grace Nail, 49
"Jumping-Off Place, The," 159–60

Kelley, Florence, 20
Kibbutzim, 170
Knapp, Adeline E. (Delle or Dora), 40, 59

Lawrence, Emmeline Pethick, 21
Leclaire, Mo., 85
Life and Labor, 47, 48
Livermore, Mary Rice, 17, 23, 41
"Living God, The," 35
Living of Charlotte Perkins Gilman, The, 30
Llano del Rio, 169
London, Jack, 47
London, England, 170
Looking Backward (Bellamy), 24–25
Lorde, Audre, 174–75
Los Angeles, Calif., 170, 175
Luther (Lane), Martha, 37

MacAvelly, Benigna, 148–49, 162, 188–89 n.7
Macnie, John, 89
"Maidstone Comfort," 159
"Making a Change," 152–53
Markham, Edwin, 44
"Martha's Mother," 148–49
Marx, Karl, and Marxism, 19, 29
Melancholia (neurasthenia), 7, 37–39, 160–62, 172–73
"Misfit, A," 27
Mitchell, S. Weir, 38, 39, 44
Montclair, N.J., 110
Morgan, Lewis Henry, 18, 50
Mothers' House, 170
Mott, Lucretia, 17
Moving the Mountain, 88–93, 99–102, 116
"Mrs. Hines' Money," 157–58
Myrdal, Alva, and Gunnar Myrdal, 170

National American Woman's Suffrage Association (NAWSA), 43, 47, 50, 52

Nationalist clubs, 24, 41, 84, 86, 122
National Woman's Christian Temperance Union (WCTU), 17
National Woman's Party (formerly the Congressional Union of NAWSA), 50
National Woman Suffrage Association, 17
Nativism, 18, 50–52
Nelson, N. O., 85
New Deal, 170
New England Kitchen, 23
New Haven, Conn., 110
New York City, 22, 23, 45, 49, 59, 88–93, 107–9, 169–70
New York Evening Post, 106
Nina West Homes, 170
Northampton, Mass., 169
Norwich Town, Conn., ix, 45, 50, 122

Oakland, Calif., 40, 46, 59
"O Heavenly World!" 81
"Old Mrs. Crosley," 153
Olerich, Henry, 24
Omniism, 123
Organicist social theory, 122–26
Our Androcentric Culture or The Man-Made World, 134
Our Brains and What Ails Them, 69
"Our Loneliness," 119
Owen, Albert, 23
Owen, Robert, 20–22, 84

Pacific Coast Women's Press Association (PCWPA), 41, 42
Pasadena, Calif., viii, ix, 39, 54
Paul, Alice, 50
Peck, Bradford, 24, 89
Peirce, Melusina (Zina) Fay, 22, 23, 63
Perkins, Frederick Beecher, 31, 32–33, 34, 68
Perkins, Mary Fitch Westcott, 31, 32, 33, 40, 68
Perkins, Thomas Adie, 31
Perkins, Thomas Gardiner, viii–ix
Pernicious Adam, 70
Philadelphia, Pa., 38–39, 170, 175

Index

Pittsburgh, Pa., 110
Providence, R.I., 33, 37, 38, 57, 58
Public Works Administration, 170

Racism, 18, 50–53, 96, 101–2, 173–75
Radburn, N.J., 170
Resettlement Administration, 170
Revolution, The, 23
Rhode Island School of Design (RISD), 33–34
Rich, Adrienne, 173, 175
Richards, Ellen Swallow, 23
Rockefeller, Laura Spellman, 169
Rodman, Henrietta, 49, 168–69
Roosevelt, Franklin Delano, 170
Ross, Edward A., 30, 43–44, 132–33
Ruskin, Tenn., 85–86, 94

St. Louis, Mo., 175
San Francisco, Calif., 32, 40, 41
Seneca Falls Conference, 17
Service house, 170
Settlement house, 20, 23–24, 42, 85
Sex differences, theories of, 131–40
Shaw, Anna Howard, 43
Shaw, George Bernard, 43
"Similar Cases," 41
Sinclair, Upton, 47
Sisters of Mercy, 175
Smith College, viii, 169
Social Darwinism, 127–30
Social ethics: CPG on race, 50–53; CPG's critique of conventional domesticity, 62–77; CPG's elitism, 53–54; CPG's implied utilitarianism, 148, 162, 188–89 n.7; CPG's informal social ethic superior to her formal, 171–75; CPG's intellectual insecurity, 6–7; CPG's philosophical commitments, 121–41; CPG's theoretical ambitions, 43–45; social ethicist in *Moving the Mountain,* 89–90
Social Gospel, 122, 129
Socialism, nonpartisan: Bellamy Nationalism, 41, 86; communitarian socialist experiments, 85–86, 94; CPG's

feminist/socialism, 29–30, 47–48; CPG's philosophical strategy for achieving, 121–41; Fabian Society, 43; and women's clubs, 18–19
"Socialist and the Suffragist, The," 48, 182 n.36
Spencer, Herbert, 25–26, 123, 127–30
Stanton, Elizabeth Cady, 17, 23, 43
Stetson, Charles Walter, 37–39, 40–41
Stetson, Katharine Beecher (Mrs. F. Tolles Chamberlin), 38, 39, 40, 45, 46, 49, 54, 59, 87
Stokes, J. G. Phelps, 123
Stowe, Harriet Beecher, 22, 23, 30, 32, 33, 83–84
Suburban greenbelt towns, 170
Sunnyside Gardens, 170
"Surplus Woman, A," 157
Sweden, 170
Sybaris (Hale), 84

Three Hundred Years Hence (Griffith), 89
"Three Thanksgivings," 158
Topolobampo, Mexico, 23
"To the Young Wife," 55
Tugwell, Rexford, 170

Uncle Tom's Cabin (Stowe), 84
Unitarianism, 29, 34, 44, 45
Unitary Household, 22
Universalism, 125–26, 171, 173–75

Vanport City, Oreg., 170

Waisbrooker, Lois, 24
Walling, William English, 47
Ward, Lester Frank, 43–44, 117, 133–36
Washington, D.C., 133
Wayland, J. A., 85
"We Stand As One," 143–44
Webb, Beatrice, and Sidney Webb, 43
West Cornwall, Conn., 169
Wharton, Edith, 39
What Diantha Did, 103, 105, 114–15, 117

Willard, Frances, 17, 41

Willowbrook Demonstration Project, 170

With Her in Ourland, 98–99, 99–102, 116

Woman movement, nineteenth and early twentieth century, 16–25, 29, 41–43, 45–54

Woman's Journal, 23, 48

Woman under Socialism (Bebel), 84–85

Women and Economics, viii, 44–45, 106, 132–33

Women's Bible project, 43

Women's clubs: a "colored" women's club, 52; CPG and, 29–42; CPG's constituency in, 86; emergence of, 17–19; heterodoxy, 49–50; in short stories, 155–58; in *What Diantha Did,* 114–15

Women's Institute for Housing and Economic Development, 175

Women's Trade Union League, 47

Woodhull, Victoria, 23

Woodhull and Claflin's Weekly, 23

Workingmen's Homes (Hale), 84

World a Department Store, The (Peck), 89

"Yellow Wallpaper, The," 44, 145

Yelping Hill, 109